fr

16 Nov 06

A Storyteller's Worlds

A family portrait shows Shlomo Noble (*seated, right*) at the age of nine or ten. The others are (*from left*) Morris, Shlomo's younger brother; Perel Peller, Grandfather David Peller's second wife; Nekha Noble, Shlomo's mother; and Miriam, Shlomo's sister.

A Storyteller's Worlds

The Education of Shlomo Noble
in Europe and America

Jonathan Boyarin

Foreword by Sander L. Gilman

Holmes & Meier
New York/London

Published in the United States of America 1994 by
Holmes & Meier Publishers, Inc.
160 Broadway
New York, NY 10038

Book design by Trudi Gershenov

This book has been printed on acid-free paper.

Library of Congress Cataloging-in-Publication Data
Noble, Shlomo, 1905–
A storyteller's worlds: the education of Shlomo Noble in Europe
and America / [interviews conducted and commented on by] Jonathan
Boyarin; foreword by Sander L. Gilman.
p.   cm. — (New perspectives)
Interviews translated from Yiddish.
Includes bibliographical references and index.
ISBN 0-8419-1343-9
1. Noble, Shlomo, 1905–   —Interviews.   2. Jews—Poland—Sanok—
Interviews.   3. Yiddishists—United States—Interviews.
4. Hasidim—Poland—Sanok—Social life and customs.   5. Immigrants—
United States—Social life and customs.   6. Sanok (Poland)—Ethnic
relations.   7. United States—Ethnic relations.   I. Boyarin,
Jonathan.   II. Title.   III. Series: New perspectives (Holmes &
Meier)
DS135.P62S1566   1994
909'.04924082'092—dc20
[B]   94-5770
CIP

Manufactured in the United States of America

Contents

Acknowledgments and Dedication

Zachary Baker, chief librarian at the YIVO Institute, provided information for several of the footnotes in this book. Krystyna Baron and Bozena Shallcross of the Polish Institute of Arts and Sciences in America helped me with Polish transcriptions. My friend and teacher Shimon Schneebalg supplied me with the Biblical, Talmudic and other rabbinic references. Work on the manuscript was completed at the Center for Studies of Social Change, New School for Social Research.

My own passion for Yiddish and the lives of its speakers was nurtured in the Jewish farm community at Farmingdale, New Jersey. As regards this book in particular, I am most grateful for the practical support and encouragement, over the course of several years, of Dr. Joe Richard and especially of Naomi Noble Richard. Therefore this book is dedicated:

To my parents, Alice and Sidney Boyarin *sheyichyu*
   and
To the memory of her parents, Nina and Shlomo Noble *aleyhem hashalom*.

Foreword

Sander L. Gilman

"*Do* I have a story for *you!?*" As we all know, storytelling is one of the most compelling means of resisting and controlling the world. It is the ultimate form of structuring memory so as to control the past. Each of us tells stories to explain to ourselves, as well as to our often involuntary listener, the way the world should have been. We have come, at the end of the twentieth century, to rely on stories about stories told to us by those our culture designates as our official storytellers. "Let me sell you a story," says the novelist; "let me tell you a hi-story," says the historian; "let me tell you about a story," says the literary critic. Each of these professional storytellers shapes the world of stories according to the designs of their professions and our need for sanitized tales, tales at least one remove from the teller.

But the storyteller's need is more visceral, more primary in its demands. It is the need to tell stories in all of the infinite variety that oral communication and repetition allows. "Let me tell you a story," states Jacob the Liar, the eponymous hero of Jurek Becker's great novel of the Shoah, while hiding and pretending to be the voice of a contraband radio. His listener, an abandoned Jewish child whom he has rescued in the ghetto, listens with intensity to a fairy tale of a princess and a cloud. "Let me tell you a story," rumbles the voice that seems to come from a radio and yet answers the child's every response. And the child who will die is suddenly free as that princess to follow her own fantasies, to be a child listening to a child's tale. But what Becker reveals is the fact that a real storyteller can't just recite tales. The real storyteller shapes his tales to his own and his listener's expectations, hones them as they are being told. The immediacy that the reader feels in this act of disguised storytelling is vital even in its reduced, literary form. The authenticity that the storyteller can claim is mirrored in this novel, and is not even distorted by the "modern" forms of mediation such as the radio. Kant claimed that truth could unfold in narration, that ideas were completed while one spoke. This is the truth of storytelling—that it is an interpersonal act, the validity of which lies in the moment of the speaker's awareness of the listener shaping the telling.

Storytelling and listening to stories as the content of storytelling is not new. Scheherazade told tales of storytellers telling tales. But in our age, a post-modern, post-Shoah, post-literate age, an age of the abstraction of storytelling, the storyteller needs to be made concrete. Storytelling in the latter half of the twentieth century seems to belong to a world of the past. Its formerly firm position in the world of culture is no longer secure. Indeed, it has begun to be displaced in its other cultural locations. The nostalgia for storytelling is so great that there is now a world of the newly professionalized storytellers who appear on the Broadway stage or in your own public library to tell tales. Storytelling as part of a psychotherapeutic milieu has been displaced by drug therapies, in which the physician does not even need to see the patient, never mind listen to the patient.

Storytelling today is a post-modern version of the storytelling of the past, a storytelling radically separate from the sharing and shaping moments of the oral tradition, an oral tradition as much at home in Talmudic disputation as in psychoanalysis. This storytelling could make a serious claim for authenticity as it demanded the full participation of the listener as well as the speaker. Today's displaced storytelling is aimed at an amorphous listener who may or may not "take part" in the act of communication. It is the presence of a "real" radio that permits us to listen but does not allow us to be part of the shaping of the tale. Indeed, even the most highly sophisticated "interactive" media, which desire to restore our presence, are only parodies of the context in which the storyteller and the listener are seated across from one another, each reading the other's expression, and gesture, and language.

Shlomo Noble's storytelling was very old-fashioned. It is old-fashioned in that it demands of its listener—Jonathan Boyarin—that he take part, that he believe, that he internalize the tale of Noble's life. And that through his very presence he help shape that narrative. This contract between listener and speaker is evident in Boyarin's own methodological discussion at the very beginning of his text. The difference between Boyarin's first account—reconstructed from his notes of that very first interview—and the later taped accounts is striking. Not because of any greater veracity of reporting in the later accounts. But because Boyarin had been made to listen and had heard so very completely during that very first meeting that he had internalized Noble's voice and Noble had captured Boyarin's fascination with his life. Boyarin comments in his opening remarks that he was amazed how accurately he had recorded that session. What he had captured, of course, was his own intense belief and role in the process of storytelling in which he—as the real, present listener—shared the authenticity of a common experience.

Now whether the content of Noble's stories is "authentic," that is, whether Noble's memories are "accurate" in the sense of a Rankean historian who needs to capture the world as it really was, is more than debatable. Who of us, at least since Goethe's autobiography, *Poetry and Truth*, can claim to separate our experiences from our desires, "poetry" from our "truths." That is not the claim for authenticity which Boyarin offers us in this text. And it is a text that reveals one of the most difficult lessons of the world after the Shoah, the difficulty of experiencing and understanding the complexity *and* the banality of Jewish life before the Shoah.

With all of the discussion of memory and its role in Jewish history, especially after the Shoah, there has been too little awareness of the role that nostalgia plays in shaping the very idea of memory. This has been the greatest error in the post-Shoah world with regard to the promise of memory as a redemptive force in the writing of history. The reception of Roman Vishniac's photographs of the world of Eastern European Jewry before the Shoah can be taken as an example of this error in processing. Here, according to the extraordinary number of reviews of Vishniac's most recent exhibition of these photographs, is the "real" world of Eastern Jewry, a world lost through the Shoah. Vishniac stood, as is evident to anyone who knows anything about the nostalgia beginning at the very turn of the century, in a long line of artists who spent their time trying to capture a vanishing world in a time of great social upheaval. Visual artists such as Hermann Struck tried to capture the vanishing *Eastern Jewish Visage*, so the title of his volume of drawings (with text by Arnold Zweig). S. An-ski, the author of the *Dybbuk*, spent 1911 to 1914 under contract, as a folklorist collecting the vanishing tales and beliefs of Eastern Jews for a major report, out of which came the *Dybbuk*. What is overlooked, of course, is that the *Dybbuk* was a Yiddish (and Russian) play written for an avant-garde theater in Vilna and that achieved world renown when performed by the avant-garde Hebrew language theater, the *Habimah*, in Moscow. The audiences for these productions were urban, middle class, acculturated (but not assimilated) Jews whose desire was to recapture a lost sense of their own authenticity.

Like Buber's Germanic retelling of Hasidic tales, Vishniac's photographs efface the world of the viewer or the reader. They do not show the banking houses of Warsaw, the factory offices of Lodz, the Jewish university or high school student organizations in Prague or Bucharest; indeed, they do not show the very world out of which came the Berlin-trained art historian, and soon to become famed scientific microphotographer, Roman Vishniac. It is a nostalgia for a world that was seen at risk—and, indeed, retrospectively was proven to be at risk. But the danger in 1900 or in 1930 or indeed in 1938 was not the Shoah—that we see only too clearly in retrospect. The anxiety during the opening decades of this century was about the loss of authenticity, about the effect of urbanization and acculturation on the very notion of the Jew. In the working through of this anxiety, East European, lower and working class, religious Jews came to represent a lost and authentic *Yiddishkayt* for the acculturated Jews of Western and Central Europe.

Shlomo Noble came to represent that "lost" tradition in the United States in a very real way. He was one of the most visible and resourceful Yiddishists in New York after the Shoah. Boyarin gives us Noble's slippery sense of himself in this dialogue (no, not in the Buberian sense—this is not a dialogue between I and thou, but a story, a story shared between you and me). Boyarin's sense of the double nature of Noble's life is reflected in Noble's narrative. Here we have a life held in suspension between the world of Eastern European Jewry perceived at risk in the 1920s and the acculturated Jewish world into which Noble flees, first in Europe and then in the United States. The new world of American Jewry, as complex and as unstable as the world from which he flees, is yet so very different in its promises. And it is this American world—the seemingly inauthentic world of Baltimore and Minneapolis—that survives the Shoah unscathed. After 1945 it is intact in all of its instability and contradictions. The world of European Jewry—from the radically assimilated to the radically separatist—has been damaged beyond belief. (But not, as shown by the resurgence of Jewish culture in contemporary Germany, destroyed.)

In this context Noble sits down with the young anthropologist Jonathan Boyarin and tells his tale—a tale of surviving, not Nazi camp guards, but the all-too-white, Anglo-Saxon professors at Johns Hopkins. And he does it in a way so as to make us understand—Boyarin allows us now to listen with him—how Noble needs to examine and understand his life. The fictionalizing of his life is not a misrepresentation. Indeed, even the double who appears to haunt Noble throughout his life in America—from his years as a college student to the appearance of the double as a cinema mogul during a stretch as a visiting professor in Los Angeles—may have been "real." But all of this complex restructuring in the act of telling has a function in framing and preserving the affective dimension, the desire and the anxiety, of Shlomo Noble's life. It is little accident that Philip Roth, without a doubt the most important American Jewish writer to come out of the East European Diaspora to which Nobel belonged, has just published *Operation Shylock*, his own account—(is it fact or fiction or both?) of his discovery of his double. This double, "Philip Roth," is living in Jerusalem and demanding that the Jews of Israel be saved from a coming Arab Shoah by being dispersed again in their traditional lands of the Diaspora—in Poland, and Russia, and Lithuania. Save us, shouts the Jew in the Diaspora, from our own anxieties about our inauthenticity. Our stories are stories about survival, not stories about destruction. Doubles belong in this world of "dybbuks," the ghosts of a lost tradition to which the modernist (and indeed, the post-modernist) writer belongs.

Nobel's storytelling stands as a "true" version of that string of novels, reaching from I. B. Singer to Philip Roth, which imagine what life for Jews in America would and could be after the Shoah. There is a sense of displacement here. We—the American Jews—have become the true heirs of Eastern European Jewry. Not the Israeli, the "tough Jew," as Paul Breines so rightly shows in his book by that name, but the Eastern Jew as writer, scholar, thinker, and storyteller. The *dugri* speech of Israeli Hebrew is not a language of storytelling—it is a language of confrontation; Yiddish was a language of negotiation, of storytelling. And it is this inheritance that marks American Jewish storytelling in all of its varieties. Boyarin's record of Noble's story of his life is an attempt to capture this quality. But it is a story that now needs to be translated from one language to another, from Yiddish to English, if not from one discourse to another. This also is a difference which is part of American Jewish culture. But why should I say any more, let him tell us a story . . .

Introduction
Pedagogic Storytelling

$\mathcal{F}$or a time my father worked as an inspector of secular education in Jewish religious schools. One day he observed a mathematics class for young children. The teacher asked one child the sum of two and two. "Four, by the grace of God," was the reply. The teacher asked another child to tell him how much six divided by three was. "Two, by the grace of God," answered the child. After the class, my father approached the teacher and said, "The children are obviously learning their lessons well. Only one thing: Were it not for the grace of God, how much would two plus two be?" "Were it not for the grace of God," the teacher responded, "there would be no telling."

—Naomi Noble Richard

$\mathcal{T}$he particular way that simple humanity and Jewishness—or any other specific identity—combine to define a person's character has much to do with the kinds of stories that person tells. Stories can be used to teach the lesson that Jews will always be burned when they rely on the fellow feeling of non-Jews, or the opposite lesson that ethnic chauvinism is a dangerous trap. They can also serve to place the listener in the situation of the story-teller, faced with the same contradictions and puzzlements the storyteller faced in an earlier historical situation, bringing home in a thousand ways the constant tensions among personal, group and human identity. When used in this dynamic way, stories broaden and deepen the world of those to whom they are told. Such are the accounts of a Jewish youth in Europe and America in the first decades of this century that Naomi Noble Richard's father, Shlomo Noble, told to me years ago, and that I in turn present in this book.

Since they refer to vanished worlds—the Hasidic Jewish communities of Galicia at the turn of the century, Johns Hopkins University in the years when it was a finishing school for the

3

sons of the Southern gentry, Los Angeles when the Brown Derby was the fashionable place to be seen—these records present in a particularly acute form a question that scholars ask about all accounts of the self. In presenting a character remaining internally coherent through the course of an often chaotic life, do they chronicle the working out in maturity of an identity shaped in childhood, or are they simultaneously the retrospective invention of an identity toward the end of life?

Shlomo Noble's account suggests some answers to these questions. The most compelling autobiographies are often those in which the protagonist begins life in a nurturing and richly particular cultural context, then withstands profound disjunctures which threaten to undermine the model for interrelation of individual and group that was instilled in childhood. The account then becomes the record of the lifelong work of creative resistance and integration, drawing on the resources of the specific childhood culture, modifying the application of its idioms, using them in ironic or subversive ways, and so forth. What we are left with is neither the unfolding of an identity given in childhood, nor the retrospective rationalization of a random series of events, but instead that part of life's work which is both *part* and *representation* of a lifelong effort to construct and preserve a particular identity.

Shlomo Noble's training in philology eventually earned him a doctorate in Germanic studies from Ohio State University in 1941. The groundwork for his rich adult career as a culture bearer and interpreter was laid in a remarkable variety of intercultural early experiences. That education, both formal and informal, is the subject of his account.

I met Shlomo Noble close to the end of nearly four decades he spent as researcher, instructor, and translator at the YIVO Institute for Jewish Research in New York City, beginning in the mid-1940s. I participated in the last formal seminar he taught, in which perhaps a *minyan* of graduate students learned to read the early Yiddish texts he had made his own scholarly specialty. In a room in what had once been the servants' floor of the Vanderbilt Mansion, we stumbled over the unfamiliar print like *heder* children learning to read for the first time. He not only tolerated but treasured some of our mistakes. One such came when I read from the Classic *Bovo Bukh*—the actual origin of the Yiddish phrase *bobbe mayse*, which has come to be understood as meaning "grandmother's stories," or old wives' tales. In its first words the author of the book announces his identity: "*Ikh, Elye Levi der shrayber*" (I, Elye Levi the writer); but I read them "*Ikh, oy vey der shrayber*" (I, woe is the writer)! Perhaps—who knows, in Noble's childhood the image would have been plausible enough—in another world this has become one of his favorite stories.

For I quickly realized that this short, unassuming, but consummately *present* person taught best when he taught his own life, re-creating scenes from the many worlds he had passed through and survived. In one class he discussed the different ways the vowel in the Yiddish word for "candle" was pronounced in different regions. "Where I came from, we pronounced it *lekht*. But when I passed through Warsaw on my way to America, I saw a storefront which bore the sign, '*do farkoyft men naft un lakht.*' I went in and asked the man, 'What does that mean— here we sell fuel and we laugh?' He was annoyed with me: 'What are you talking about—*lakht* means candles!'"

I had come to study Yiddish because somehow, in my own childhood, I had been possessed by a desperate nostalgia for the unknown world out of which the language came. The stories of Sholem Aleichem and the panorama of *Fiddler on the Roof* simply were not enough to satisfy that nostalgia. It took sustained contact with people who had come from that place and time. I was searching for someone who knew how to create in word images a bridge across the gulf that separated my origins from hers or his—someone who could make me imagine myself in that world.

Shlomo Noble was the person I found. The echoes and surprises and ironies that make the world a place worth entering each morning were for him contained, above all, in language. He was an old-fashioned scholar, but not an "objective" one, since he knew that it is unnecessary and often impossible to separate neatly the language one *studies* from the language in which one studies. His worlds were molded, linked, and separated by language, both spoken and written. Thus, whenever he retold a story about one of those worlds, it literally became present again. In the process of telling these stories, he also gave me precious tools for the creation of my own Jewish worlds. Over the past decade I have retold these stories countless times, and my aim in making this book is to pass on the gift to you.

Shlomo Noble's record, of course, is also a facet of the struggle for identity of an entire people in the twentieth century. That collective search for identity has been tortured by the experience of genocide. But it has also been rendered almost impossible because of the false terms in which it has been framed: the terms of a choice between fidelity and rationality, between the particular and the universal. Noble's synthesis of the scholarly and the personal in the form of pedagogic storytelling anticipates the present critique of the dichotomy between subjective cultural involvement and objective, detached reasoning. His Jewish "trickster" stories suggest that a person need not choose between denying a specific group identity and being stifled by that identity. His narrative connects us to the successive worlds in which he lived: the Galician *shtetl* attempting to hold onto old ways in the face of the dislocations of war; the new social movements responding to the problems and opportunities of independent Poland; the attempt to establish Orthodox Jewish life and learning in the immigrant Lower East Side; small-town American Jewish life; American universities in the years before World War II; and the curious encounters of a secular scholar of Jewish studies. Noble thus moved from a highly conservative,

Torah-oriented worldview to one dominated by the scholarly and worldly spirit of "the science of Judaism." The journey from Europe to America took him across a cultural ocean as well, one he remained acutely aware of and comments on in his narrative. Yet his academic professional work in America never became fully divorced from the world into which he had been born; the synthesis of the two made him a true storyteller—the kind who connects us in a unique way to a world we might otherwise truly have lost.

World War I has almost disappeared from collective Jewish memory, but the Jews of Europe experienced it as one of the greatest catastrophes in their history. Entire communities were uprooted, and their ways of life never returned to "normal." During the two decades that followed, new possibilities opened up even as the threat of a greater disaster loomed larger and larger. The map of Eastern Europe had been thoroughly reinvented, and Jews experienced new political and social aspirations. Because of the Nazi genocide, the path they traced in their attempt to reconcile Jewish identity with modernity reached a dead end. Almost: the testimony of Jews like Shlomo Noble who were born into the traditional world at the beginning of this century and lived on after the destruction can help us to retrace that path in memory.

What was destroyed by World War I? What was made possible by the breaking of traditional constraints on the individual? How can we comprehend the experiences and responses of Jews and of others in Europe and North America in the first half of our century?

Such questions are certainly of concern to historians and anthropologists. Both kinds of scholars deal with sets of relations that were especially strained in the interwar period: between tradition and innovation; between a sense of home and the pull away from home exerted by larger economic forces; between group identity and individual autonomy; between our helpless involvement in a history we hardly determine, and our ideal of personal responsibility for the course of our lives. Furthermore, historians and anthropologists are reaching a consensus that the nature of the record itself—and not just what it tells us about the "reality" supposed to lie behind it—is an integral part of any investigation. This new awareness has come about largely because the very possibility of one individual's conveying her or his experience to another is in question. No less a thinker than Walter Benjamin even claimed that our doubts in this sphere are largely a result of World War I itself:

> Was it not noticeable at the end of the war that men returned from the battlefield grown silent—not richer, but poorer in communicable experience? What ten years later was poured out in the flood of war books was anything but experience that goes from mouth to mouth.[1]

Benjamin's point about the dehumanization of mass trench warfare reminds us that World War I stands not merely as a convenient way to divide historical epochs, but as a fundamental event with repercussions for our own possible forms of experience. And it is precisely during World War I that the account contained in this book commences. Thus, Shlomo Noble's narrative presented here—which I collected in nine hours of oral interviews, plus notes taken from one preliminary interview—is in a sense not only a record, but an act: communication despite history.[2]

"Oral history" is often seen as giving a voice to those who are unable to wield their own pens, but Noble was anything but a naive informant. He knew very well how to communicate his intended lessons in cultural history. In the pages below, I will concentrate on an analysis of Noble's rhetorical technique, reflections on the relation between the taped and written versions of his account, ethnohistorical highlights of the text and how these are integrated, through the presentation of Noble as a character, into his narrative.

This account of Noble's education is not a life history. Thus, for example, there are no references to his mother after his emigration from Europe, although she did indeed join him and his father in America. Noble never announced that he was going to concentrate on his education, but it was characteristic for him to do so. His narrative reflects his childhood studies with *melamdim*, old-fashioned European Hebrew teachers. His 1941 Ohio State University dissertation on *khumesh-taytsh*, the traditional lexicon of teachers' glosses of the Bible into Yiddish, dealt as does this narrative with the linked themes of language, education and communication. Education, finally, involves both the imposition of arbitrary cultural systems within relations of unequal power[3] and the transmission of precious memories and insights to a new generation. Expressing critical judgments on the forms and content of tradition without repudiating the memory of its bearers calls for a modern-day trickster. That, I will argue, is perhaps the best way to describe the Shlomo Noble who emerges in these stories.

According to the title of a recent book by David Lowenthal, the past is a foreign country.[4] If so, then Noble recollecting his life history is in a position analogous to that of an ethnographer studying his own culture. The way in which ethnographers justify, through appeal to the experience of participant observation, their literary conceit of "speaking for the natives" has come under immense scrutiny lately. The situation of a scholarly memoirist gives the issue a different twist. Of the recollecting subject and the subject who is recollected, which is the "insider" and which the "outsider"? The youth had an immediate experience upon which the elder imposes "foreign" categories of understanding. On the other hand, the elder is the actor, while the account of his own youth is a product of his need for an image of a meaningful life. Actually, both subjects refuse to be pinned down in this fashion. It is useful to talk of them sometimes as though they were separate entities, but in fact what we are witnessing is the self-fashioning of one Shlomo Noble; and although we may continue to wonder about inside and outside, as on a Möbius strip, actually there is only a single surface.

This self-fashioning proceeds by way of constant cultural strategizing on Noble's part. As a scholar, he is like an explorer of a vanished world returning with a chart of the path between that world and this one. His desire for an image of himself as a coherent, autonomous individual throughout his picaresque experiences demands that he record the way his native culture represses the anarchic individual; the way the dominant culture represses the anarchic individual; and the way the dominant culture represses his native culture. At the same time, he is a survivor and witness to the vanished world, and his almost total power to shape its image requires of him that it be represented with love modeled on the divine.

How better to achieve all this than through the stance of the trickster? "Trickster" is a figure appropriated by scholars from the culture of North American Indians, but also a type represented more or less exactly in tales told throughout the world. Tricksters serve in essence to keep people from being totally taken in by their own cultures, including cultural claims to transcend mortality. They are an escape valve, always "on the other hand," or, in cultures used to dialectical reasoning, sometimes "on the third hand." They may represent the weak, whose wit can at times achieve ambiguous victories against the power of the strong. They can make ironic comments and even turn things entirely upside down without losing their place in the social world. Stories about tricksters are especially beloved, since they tell us what is particular about the symbolic world of a given group of people without divorcing those symbols from the problems people face in daily life. Societies with no room for tricksters and their stories are in trouble. When tricksters lose their balance and sink into chaos, as happens with some of the incidental characters in this narrative, it is likewise an indication of malaise in their society.[5]

Nowhere in his account does Noble speak of the trickster theme directly. However, I think his theory about the particular cultural insights available to those on the margins of society (see his account of his stay in Minnesota) is relevant here. Noble documents his loss of traditional faith, but he never lost his love of Jewish learning. He was not a man caught between two worlds, or in transition from one to the other. His place, like the trickster's, was at the margin, and his task was to blur the boundary between inside and outside.

All of the interviews were conducted in Yiddish. The body of this book is, then, an edited version of a simultaneous transcription from tape and translation into English from Yiddish. The tapes were made during the spring of 1981. The sessions were held at my request. My friend Charles Nydorf, then a graduate student in linguistics at Columbia University who had also studied with Noble, was also present. I thought of asking Dr. Noble for his reminiscences because in my studies with him at YIVO, I had found that vignettes (or in Yiddish *masholim*, a word which helpfully connotes both "examples" and "parables") were his favorite technique for conveying the cultural and linguistic history that were his scholarly concern.

Certainly these tapes are one of those precious links of "oral history" which represent a kind of levee against the flood of oblivion. The storytelling mode itself recalls a time when, or so we imagine, the chains of orally transmitted memory tended to be elaborated rather than severed, as today. In his formal research, Shlomo Noble was generally a philologist, a cultural historian on the nineteenth-century German model. But Noble's storytelling scholarship, as represented here, also fits well within a narrative trend that has become prominent in recent cultural studies.

My motivation to record Shlomo Noble's stories may have been influenced by this new trend, but his scholarship probably was not. In fact, given his grounding in linguistics and the decades in which he was a producing scholar, we would expect his teaching to reflect the scientific bias of structuralism, which strips stories down to their "basic elements" and removes the suspense and surprises that make a tale a wonder.[6]

By contrast, Shlomo Noble's corpus of memories does not separate out narrative from analysis, or change over time from the structures which make sense of change. His account is remarkably free of twin and opposite dangers faced by memoirists born into intimate, traditional communities: on the one hand, sentimentalization of his childhood world, and on the other, devaluation of the supposedly "naive" past through the prism of the Enlightenment. And yet Shlomo Noble most certainly was a secular scholar. His emphasis on an intersubjective approach which allowed people he had known to "speak to" his students does not prevent him from presenting himself as an autonomous, judging persona in his narrative. There are indications in the text which help explain this synthesis of empathy and critique.

Often Noble's memories hinge on a single word, and the consequential place it occupied at a critical moment in his or someone else's life. Many of these words are discussed in the commentaries I provide after each chapter, but let me list a few of them here. There is the name of the city of Radziwilow in the Ukraine, which appears and reappears when it's least expected, thus helping to hold this highly episodic narrative together. There is Noble's first encounter with the unsettling concept of a "valentine." The Polish word "*nashe*," being "ours," bears a heavy burden of irony. In these cases, respect for the specificity of the word and the concept encountered in the unpredictable course of life is combined with a lesson about how that word serves to mark boundaries.

Noble is fascinated by his own and others' naiveté and misinterpretations of language, as well as the power and risk that language use entails. Among the techniques he uses to bring together the language of his story with the situation he recounts are substitutions of words to mirror substitutions of persons (see the account of his Bar Mitzvah); borrowing from the linguistic idiosyncrasies of one of his characters to enliven an entirely different story (follow him to the *furnitsur shtor*); and dramatizing the danger of confusing sacred hymns with schoolyard rhymes (in Chapter 4).

Noble also knew the disruptive and dangerous potentials inherent in the relation between spoken and written language. In an anecdote that forms part of his description of his yeshiva years in New York, he meets the threat of a young woman's challenge—"If not now, when?"—by transforming it into an utterly conventionalized homily. Later on at Johns Hopkins University, he recites ad nauseam the *Oxford English Dictionary*'s definition of "apocryphal," using pedantry as a weapon against an authority figure whom he believes to be discriminating against him.

Thus Noble builds his account, from single words to coherent descriptions of different cultural worlds. My subsequent task has been to translate Noble's account into a version that works as written storytelling, while retaining at least some of the dense historical resonance of the language he used.

I am convinced that once he agreed to this project, Shlomo Noble began to plan his narratives. I tried once or twice to have him answer standardized questions, such as "I'm interested in the domestic lifeways. A day in Sanok." On that occasion he replied politely but not in detail, and the transcript makes it clear that my question was an intrusion into his story.

Noble's clear narrative intent places me—as auditor, translator, transcriber, and finally editor of the tapes—in a distinctive position relative to other scholars who have produced "oral histories" or "dialogic ethnographies." Bonnie Smith's *Confessions of a Concierge*, for example, is an entertaining and informative slice of twentieth-century French social history. Smith freely acknowledges that she "actually pieced together" Mme Lucie's autobiographical account "from the higgledy-piggledy order in which she told her story."[7] On the opposite end of the dilemma between editing and *verité*, Kevin Dwyer's *Moroccan Dialogues* is virtually nothing but a translated transcript of a series of formal interviews with a fairly representative Moroccan male, preceded by an extended theoretical justification of Dwyer's procedure.[8] Because of Noble's skill as a storyteller and experience as a teacher, neither rearrangement on the scale Smith found necessary nor an introduction as detailed as Dwyer's is necessary here. Yet publication of a raw transcript would have been a disservice to Noble, since the way he told stories was based on a balance between fidelity and communication. Failure to edit at all would have greatly diminished his capacity, through me, to communicate with readers.

Almost a year passed between my completion of the transcript and my first rough edit. During that time, I hoped to produce some sort of notation scheme to indicate where I had made changes. Such a system, to be determined in advance, would have permitted an exact mapping between the transcript and the published text. But the system did not come to me. Then, in the summer of 1988, I heard two lectures by Professor Robert Stepto of Yale University. One was on oral folk sources in Zora Neale Hurston's ethnography and fiction. The other, on "fraternal narratives," discussed the relations between three male black writers and the subjects of their biographical accounts. I thought that if anyone would understand my editing dilemma, it was Professor Stepto. When I asked him for guidelines he might suggest, his advice was simple: "Just keep asking yourself as you're going along: Am I being a good brother?"

It is, therefore, the sense of relation (as both kinship and telling) that has guided my editorial hand. I do not mean to mystify the process, and I will discuss certain issues that illuminate both Noble's practical strategy and mine. But such a discussion will not establish the kind of "scientific" method I had originally hoped for. I would like to share some sense of my own experi- ence during the editing phase, and to prepare the reader to be on the lookout for those "traces of spoken language" that Noble used so effectively, and that I have intentionally retained.

A preliminary task is to determine exactly what to include. Noble actually spoke during ten sessions. Because of an oversight on my part, I failed to record the first one, and instead took detailed notes immediately after the interview. Yet the work of interpretation starting with a set of notes like this is quite differ- ent from that of a transcribed and translated oral recording. In a way the notes are already mine, not Noble's, and many of the qualms about reordering, removal of redundancies and the like which I am faced with when considering the transcript did not give me pause in "writing up" these notes. The style of this chapter may therefore be taken as an example of the "as told to" genre, which is all too often presented as autobiography, even in scholarly presentations.

There is also material that was included on the tapes but that Noble may have considered incidental, not intended for poster- ity. In fairness to his intention, perhaps this material should be excluded from the book; but in at least one case, which I will discuss, the incidental point sets such a pregnant framework for the session's main narrative that I find it indispensable.

Stepto's advice to "be a good brother" confirmed my suspicion that the criteria and method for transforming a transcription into a publishable text cannot be whittled down to a system. On one hand there is a temptation to remove the voice of the interviewer—who is also the first audience. The critic Dennis Tedlock warns against this tendency:

> Those who make written documents from tape-recorded discourse have a strong tendency to get swept away in the monological currents of writing;

Edward Ives, in *The Tape-Recorded Interview*, makes it an explicit rule of transcription that an English-language narrator's "you know" and "you see," along with an interviewer's "sure" and "I see," should all be edited out.[9]

To have eliminated all of Charles Nydorf's and my interjections, Noble's asides to us, and so forth would thus be to erase the traces of interaction, whereas to preserve all of them faithfully would be a pedantic imposition on readers' patience. The ones I have retained are generally points where meaning is being collectively created, as when I ask the meaning of *zkhus ovos.* Nydorf says, "The merit of . . ." and Noble concludes, "the fathers." But this is an extremely loose guideline. The esthetics of editing imply negotiation at each point between the demands of content and the demands of transmission.

Aside from elimination of some of his listeners' interjections, redundant phrasing, a few brief passages which I could not understand, and most of the material that was included on the tapes but was not part of his intended narrative, relatively more drastic editorial decisions I have taken are of the following order:

1. Certain spots—especially those which need to convey relatively specialized information about Jewish culture—have been reorganized for easier comprehension by the reader. (One such is the story about Noble's brother's interpretation of the Talmudic passage *hoyo roykhev al gabe beheyme.*)

2. I have placed in italics words or phrases that Noble spoke in a language, such as English, other than the language of that particular story only when I determined that the switch conveyed significant meaning. I have already referred to several such examples and discuss them at greater length after the various chapters.

3. In one instance, I have put an entire sentence into Noble's mouth for the sake of continuity. That sentence is "But there are a few things I want to tell you about before we leave the yeshiva for good."

4. The chapter divisions, titles and subheadings are mine.

5. Whether because of our eagerness to hear the Flayshman story, or because it fit well into Noble's schedule to tell it on that particular day, he actually told it to us in between his account of his year at Johns Hopkins and his account of the rest of his higher education. I have moved it to the end, both to provide a more natural sequence to the story of his schooling and because it constitutes the book's most memorable material.

6. The final tape, discussing his years at YIVO, has been eliminated entirely, largely because he requested that we keep much of what he told us in confidence. This material is included in the copy of the transcript which I have given to the YIVO archives.

As I have suggested, one theme running through Noble's discourse is the ceaseless complementarity and mutual betrayal of the oral and the written. In fact, at points Noble's narrative style seems to borrow from that of the *melamed*, that oral expounder of written texts. And just as writing both reduces and reshapes an oral communication, oral exposition "speaks in" features missing from a written text.

I have left in references to external events and popular culture (the year of President McKinley's assassination, Joe Namath's birthplace, the cartoon character Barney Google). These interrupt the narrative, but they also anchor it and provide points of contact to a common store of everyday knowledge shared by Noble, his interviewers and his readers.

Some of Noble's techniques which may be "good speaking," as Tedlock says, run the risk of coming across as "bad writing" if left pristine, for example: "and several roads led into the market, various roads led into the market, and the Gentiles came there on Fridays, on the roads, and every Gentile came with a wagon . . ." In oral storytelling this repetition reinforces the idea that this was the routine, the pattern. It also gives the listener more time to develop the mental image the storyteller is trying to evoke.

On a few occasions I felt I could trace specific meaning in Noble's gaps and redundancies, and so I left them as they were. Thus, in a discussion of the growth of anti-Semitism in post-World War I Poland, he says "And there began a political, a political . . ." He need not inform us once again that he is talking about anti-Semitism; instead he can emphasize its novelty as a political movement. In some instances, again, I have left in Noble's apparently superfluous question to us, "Do you understand?" because the rhythmic pause has the effect of building suspense.

An empathetic rather than logical understanding of vignettes told from memory is, of course, more likely when there is already a strong personal relationship between the storyteller and his audience. Shlomo Noble called us—graduate students in linguistics, literature, social sciences—*kinder*, as if we were truly small children and he were our *melamed*. The transcript contains numerous forms of linkage among the storyteller, the story and the audience. There is the connection established between two chains of oral memory, as when Noble refers to his uncle who had been in America so long that he had voted for McKinley—*er hot gevut far McKinley*,[10] and Nydorf remarks that his grandfather remembered McKinley's death. There is use of an object in the room—in this case, me—as a prop, when Noble says that the Ukrainians had "long hair, long hair. Like, for example, you—and even longer." (This example points out the often obscured fact that the researcher also changes from the time an account is recorded to the time it is publicly presented. Today I would be useless as an illustration of the Ukrainians' long hair.) There is complicity among the storyteller and his audience, as when Noble recounted a nasty trick played on a young man, and scolded us for being amused—"Why are you laughing?"—only to start laughing himself.

Another aspect of Noble's sophisticated teaching was his acute sense of interlinguistics and his employment of multilingual referents. Often phrases and words in English, Hebrew, Ukrainian or German are interjected so subtly as to seem mere interferences with Noble's native Yiddish. In many cases, however, their use bears a precise narrative meaning. The first example of this occurs right after Noble's description in chapter 2 of "an old settlement"—a long-established, stable community. Noble expresses in English the reaction of Galician Jews who went to big cities as refugees during World War I: "Cheer up, old boy. [Why should I be] Careful? Nobody knows me around here." The fact that this is enunciated in a language other than Yiddish already underscores the anomie Jews felt in this situation. The fact it is in English foreshadows the way he himself was to shed traditional scruples in the American context.

Noble's concern for effective teaching through storytelling is explicitly evident at several points. Especially in the early sessions, he frequently stopped to make sure we understood various words and phrases. And in the course of describing how the Jews of his town foiled a planned pogrom, he stops twice to ask us: "Do you see by now what happened?" "*Nu*—do you see the plan yet, or don't you see it yet?" On the one hand he is checking whether we are following the logic of the story. On the other, he is challenging us to replicate the logic of the story—to place ourselves in the predicament of the Jewish community and imagine the solution they invented. His questions to us are simultaneously a test and a technique for increasing dramatic tension. They help to join the horizon of the Jewish community—the collective protagonist of this episode—with the horizon of his audience.

Several times Noble lingers on his attraction to the Gentile world, his flattery at an offer of adoption into a Southern gentry family, his misgivings about the ignorance, censorship and hypocrisy plaguing Jewish life in America. Yet Noble neither forgot his past nor compartmentalized his identity. I believe one way he was able to maintain a balance was through his pursuit not so much of *Wissenschaft des Judentums*—the German phrase means "the science of Judaism"—but rather of *Yidishe visnshaft*, the Yiddish phrase which I use here to mean critical scholarship in his native language. The importance of the language of scholarship is brought out eloquently by Walter Ong, who writes:

> It would appear likely that a textualized, chorographically controlled language such as Learned Latin aided greatly in establishing the distance between the observer and the observed, between the knower and the known, that science, and especially modern science, required. No longer a mother tongue, Learned Latin left all its users free of the rich, emotional, unconscious, but often confusingly subjective involvements of a language learned orally from infancy . . .[11]

While Noble was careful to learn modern European languages well, he had no need or wish to be free of the "subjective involvements" in his mother tongue. For Noble, learned Latin and all the other tools of secular scholarship he mastered were used not to escape childhood associations but rather to bridge the gaps between all of his worlds. This account in turn invites us, as readers, to join in that subjective yet critical involvement, through a record which demands our close attention and our active imagination. We may go on to tell some of these stories ourselves, to our friends, our children, our students. But equally important, the stories Shlomo Noble tells in this book hint at ways that we may perceive and communicate our own worlds more fully.

Notes

1. From Walter Benjamin, "The Storyteller," in *Illuminations* (New York: Schocken Books, 1969), p. 84. For a discussion of this theme in Yiddish literature, see David Roskies, *Against the Apocalypse: Responses to Catastrophe in Jewish Literature* (Cambridge, Mass: Harvard University Press, 1984).

2. The entry under "act" in the *Oxford Etymological Dictionary* reveals that the term historically covered both speech and other kinds of doing. There is a similar link between the older Hebrew *ma'asa* ("deed") and the Yiddish *mayse* ("story"). J. L.

Austin's study of *How to Do Things with Words* (Cambridge, Mass: Harvard University Press, 1962), much as it has taught us, may mask the historical process of the *separation* of speech from other kinds of doing.

3. See Pierre Bourdieu and Jean-Claude Passeron, *Reproduction in Education, Society and Culture* (London and Beverly Hills: Sage Publications, 1977).

4. *The Past Is a Foreign Country* (New York: Cambridge University Press, 1984).

5. The classic citation on the trickster figure is Paul Radin's *The Trickster* (London: Routledge and Kegan Paul, 1956). On elderly Jews as tricksters, see Jack Kugelmass, *The Miracle of Intervale Avenue* (New York: Schocken Books, 1986), p. 223n. My notion of the trickster as a strategist finessing the choice between cultural ossification and cultural oblivion is indebted to Gerard Vizenor's experimental fiction *The Trickster of Liberty* (Minneapolis: University of Minnesota Press, 1988). For a discussion of the possibilities of "trickster scholarship" in feminist criticism, see Naomi Schor, "Reading Double: Sand's Difference," in *The Poetics of Gender*, ed. Nancy K. Miller (New York: Columbia University Press, 1986), pp. 248–69.

6. That style of structural analysis applied to orally collected texts has been severely criticized by Dennis Tedlock, a partisan of the recent dialogic, narrative trend in ethnography. Tedlock writes: ". . . the French structuralists . . . limit the native to a narrative or 'diachronic' function and leave the analytic or 'synchronic' function to themselves. In effect, the collected texts are treated as if they were raw products, to which value is then added by nomenclature." *The Spoken Word and the Work of Interpretation* (Philadelphia: University of Pennsylvania Press, 1983), p. 237.

7. New Haven: Yale University Press, 1985, p. xviii.

8. Baltimore: Johns Hopkins University Press, 1982.

9. *The Spoken Word and the Work of Interpretation*, p. 288n.

10. Instead of the standard Yiddish verb *shtimen* ("to vote"), he substitutes *vutn*—obviously a relic of immigrant Yiddish. By thus adopting his uncle's precise dialect, we may say that Noble makes his statement in the grammatical third person but the lexical first person.

11. "Orality, Literacy and Medieval Textualization," *New Literary History* 16:1–2, at p. 9.

1

The First Interview

January 30, 1981

$\mathcal{G}$ spent my childhood in the town of Sanok, on the River San in eastern Galicia. The peasants living on the east bank of the river were Ukrainians, while those on the west bank were Poles. The town was built on the mountainside, and there was a railroad station in the valley. The population of the town was equally divided among Poles, Ukrainians and Jews. Jews from many places had come to live there, on account of the railroad-car factory located in Sanok. All of them were Hasidim. There were twenty Hasidic prayerhouses, including those of the Belzer, Sadigerer, and Sandzer Hasidim. All of these groups had their own dialects of Yiddish.

My grandfather, David Peller, was born in 1852. His daughter, my mother, was the sixth child born to her parents, and the first to live—after a blessing to this effect had been secured from the Sandzer Rebbe.[1] I myself was born in 1905, one week before Passover.[2]

1. Reb Chaim Halberstam (1793–1876), author of several books called *Divrey Chaim*, dealing with ritual purity and divorce laws, responsa and sermons on Torah and festivals.
2. According to Naomi Noble Richard, Noble's secular birthday was July 4. It is

My mother's mother died before I was born. My grandfather was very fond of swimming, and used to swim in the river when he went to the ritual bath on Friday afternoons. One day while my grandfather was at the bath, someone told my grandmother that he had drowned. She suffered a heart attack, lived for a year longer and then died.

My step-grandmother Perel was a true woman of the people. There were many Gypsies in the region she came from, and she had learned their language. She taught me several words, some songs and other Gypsy folklore, but I don't remember any of it. Who knew then what would be significant now?

My grandfather was a Sandzer Hasid, and I do remember some of the stories that he told me about the Rebbe. One day while the Rebbe was holding court, a poor water carrier came in and complained that he was so poor he couldn't buy new boots, that his boots were nothing but holes. What should he do? The Rebbe—who was lame—got up out of his chair and limped angrily toward the water carrier: "What? There's a God in heaven, a merciful Father, and you come to me, a weak thing of flesh and blood who is likely to be dead tomorrow, asking for favors?" The Rebbe slipped him secretly a ten-ruble note, shouting, "Next time you want something, ask God for it!" Shortly thereafter the Rebbe died.

I myself am named for the grandson of Reb Chaim Sandzer, the first Bobover Rebbe.[3]

I began going to *heder*, the traditional Jewish school, when I was five years old, just after moving to Sanok from a small town nearby. My mother had to pick me up from heder, because I was too young to walk home alone. First we were taught the alphabet. I learned fast, and was taught to read the Hallel.[4] I read one

possible that my notes or Noble's account was inaccurate. However, it is tempting to think that his "secular birthdate" was bestowed on him at Ellis Island.

3. Lived 1847–1906. The Bobover Hasidim, now headed by that first rebbe's elderly grandson, are one of the largest Hasidic groups in America today.

4. A sequence of several Psalms traditionally recited on holidays, at the new moon and certain other momentous occasions.

verse without knowing what it meant, and burst into tears because of the sound of the words. I couldn't explain to the teacher
why I was upset; I didn't even know the word for "sound." The
teacher suggested to my mother that I might not be a very good
student, since I cried for no reason. This is my first memory.

My grandfather was a businessman. He lost and made substantial sums several times. Once, when he made a good sum, he
decided to make a pilgrimage to all of the places mentioned in
the book *Kahal Hasidim* as having been visited by the Baal Shem
Tov.[5] I've retained two stories that he told me from that trip:

One day my grandfather was passing through a small peasant
village where no Jews lived, near the town of Kossov. He realized it was time to say the afternoon prayers, and looked for a
place where he could wash his hands. He asked a peasant if there
was a stream or a well nearby. The peasant said yes—right over
there was "Sruel's well." It had wonderful healing properties. If
a person was sick, they could come there and drink, and they
would be healed. The same thing with a horse, *lehavdil*,[6] if it was
lame, or a child. The story goes that once, while Israel[7] Baal
Shem Tov was on one of his rapturous meditative walks through
the forest, he struck the ground with his stick and that well burst
forth. Since then, everyone around had regarded it as having
magic properties.

My grandfather's journey also took him to the city of Berdichev. Once he entered a synagogue where a group of men were
about to sit down and study a passage in the Gemore, the Baby-
lonian Talmud. A sooty chimney sweep came in and went into
a side room. A few minutes later a man in clean clothes came
in, sat down and led the study session. Afterwards my grandfather asked what had happened to the chimney sweep. It turned

5. The founder of the modern Hasidic movement.
6. Literally, "to make a distinction." Traditional Yiddish speakers use this term
when a suggested comparison—as here between humans and horses—might seem an
indecent denigration of one of the items referred to.
7. The southern Yiddish pronunciation of the name "Israel" is "Yisruel" or
"Sruel" for short.

out that he had been the one leading the study session. My grandfather told this story to illustrate the holiness of Berdichev, where a chimney sweep could also be a scholar, and also the fact that Berdichev was a completely Jewish town, where the police and all the functionaries and workers as well were Jewish.

During World War I my father was drafted into the Austro-Hungarian Army, along with many other fathers in the town. Thus there was no one around to examine their young sons every Sabbath and see how they were progressing in their studies. My grandfather moved to town from the village where he lived, so that he could supervise my education. He established a society of men who collectively saw to the weekly examination of all the heder boys, each student being assigned to a particular member of the society. I was assigned to the rabbinical judge, the *dayan*. I looked forward to the examination each week, because if I did well I got Sabbath fruit—one raisin and a piece of dried apple, a great treat. The society wanted to make sure that none of the *melamdim*, the Jewish schoolteachers, were slacking off. If too many children of a particular melamed didn't do well in their examinations on a particular Sabbath, the members of the society would go to that *melamed* and tell him to start working more diligently with the children.

When the Russians entered Sanok during World War I, practically everybody left the town. My family, including my grandfather and me, left as well, but we couldn't walk very fast, and the Russians caught up with us. We decided to turn back. On the way back, we came to a place where there was a big puddle, and Cossacks who were passing by decided to ride through and spatter mud all over us. For the first time I understood the saying "A Jew is in exile." The soldiers who came after the Cossacks were from deep inside Russia, didn't know anything about Jews and weren't anti-Semitic.

One day my grandfather and I had to go down to the railroad station, and we stopped into a small prayer room for the afternoon and evening prayers. While we were there one Hasid started counting the *Omer*[8] very loudly, using a Hebrew pronunciation that I found very strange. He added *h*'s where they weren't written in, pronounced the vowels differently, and so forth. I asked my grandfather, "Doesn't that Jew know Hebrew?" My grandfather rebuked me, telling me not to make fun, because that was the way they spoke Hebrew where that man came from. For me, this was an early lesson in cultural relativism.

Our own synagogue had a choir made up of young boys who sang along with the cantor. I was the shortest of the boys, and got to stand on the top step of the *bime*, the platform in the center where the service was conducted. On Hanukkah, the choir used to go around to all of the rich men in town and sing traditional Hanukkah songs, and we would receive Hanukkah money in return.

It happened that on Rosh Hashanah of 1914 an Austrian regiment from Vienna marched into the town square. They were given leave, but when they started walking around they were amazed to see that all of the stores in town were closed on a Wednesday. An officer went up to a Jew who happened to be passing by and asked him why. The Jew explained that it was a very holy day for the Jews, and the officer asked if he could go into the synagogue and listen to the service. He went in and was very impressed by the cantor. After the service he approached the cantor, congratulated him, said that he himself was a composer and asked in what conservatory the cantor had studied. The cantor didn't understand. The officer explained, "What music school?" The cantor said, "*Baym rebens tish*," at the rebbe's table: he just listened to all of the various melodies that were composed and sung by the Hasidic rebbes and their followers.

I also have clear memories of Purim in Sanok. The rabbi

8. The daily marking, prescribed by the Torah, of the passing of the forty-nine days between Passover and Shavuot, which commemorates the giving of the Torah at Mount Sinai.

would be honored with the most coveted portion of the Torah reading, and after he made the blessing, he would announce that he was renouncing his post. Then a certain Jew, whose grandchildren now live in Riverdale, would come up and say that he was going to be the rabbi now. He delivered all sorts of humorous interpretations of the traditional texts. Here was one little Purim skit:

A man comes into the synagogue and asks the superintendent to let him see some of the old religious books (there was an ancient Jewish library there). The superintendent would ask: "What's your name?"

"Moshe."

"Which Moshe?"

"Moshe ben Amram" (the Prophet Moses). [Noble picks up Barron's outline of European literature which lies on his desk, and leafs through to illustrate.]

The superintendent is astounded: usually when someone asks to see a book, he sits down and studies it properly. Moses explains that he's heard about all of these thousands of books that are supposed to be *Toyres Moyshe*, the teachings of Moses, but after looking through these, he sees that they have absolutely nothing to do with what he wrote! This was a ritually sanctioned criticism of all of the extra laws which have been added to the Five Books by the rabbis through the centuries, in the name of the Torah of Moses.[9]

9. This vignette in turn rests on a story in the Talmud (Menachot 29b) which in effect sanctions innovations made by scholars in later generations:

Reb Judah said in the name of Rav, When Moses ascended on high he found the Holy One, blessed be He, engaged in affixing coronets to the letters. Said Moses, "Lord of the Universe, Who stays Thy hand?" He answered, "There will arise a man, at the end of many generations, Akiba ben Joseph by name, who will expound upon each tittle heaps and heaps of laws." "Lord of the Universe," said Moses, "permit me to see him." He replied, "Turn thee round." Moses went and sat down behind eight rows and listened to the discourses upon the law. Not being able to follow their arguments he was ill at ease, but when they came to a certain subject and the disciples said to the master, "Whence do you know it?" and the latter replied, "It is a law given unto Moses at Sinai," he was comforted. Thereupon he returned to the Holy One, blessed be He, and said, "Lord of the Universe, Thou hast such a man and

The Sanok bathhouse had a top floor for men and a bottom floor for women. On Purim they would tell a story about a man who comes to the bathhouse keeper and says, "Every week for years I've been giving money for repairs to the bathhouse. But today there was a loose board, and when I stepped on it, I fell right through into the women's section!"

A third man, listening to the conversation, replies: "Tell me where the board is!"

The story is pointed in two ways: it teases the trustees by suggesting that they pocket the money that's donated for the upkeep of the bathhouse, and also suggests salacious motives on the part of men who are supposed to be going to purify themselves.

The Jews in Sanok spoke Yiddish, but language was a contentious issue. In 1910 the Austro-Hungarian Government decided to do a census. They wanted to have an ethnic count of the population, so everyone had to put down their native language. The choices included Ukrainian, Polish, Hungarian, German and a few others. At the bottom, it said that it was a crime to put down any other language. A leading Yiddishist argued to the Jews, "If you put down Ukrainian, the Poles will get angry; and if you put down Polish, you'll only anger the Ukrainians. On the other hand, if you put down German, you're simply not telling the truth, because you speak Yiddish." Masses of Jews actually did put down Yiddish, and half the town was thrown into jail with a six-week sentence. Eventually the government realized that was ridiculous, and let everybody out.

On the other hand, it must be said that the boundaries be-

Thou givest the Torah by me!" He replied, "Be silent, for such is My decree." Then said Moses, "Lord of the Universe, Thou hast shown me his Torah, show me his reward." "Turn thee round," said He; and Moses turned round and saw them weighing out his flesh at the market stalls after Rabbi Akiba's martyrdom. "Lord of the Universe," cried Moses, "such Torah, and such a reward!" He replied, "Be silent, for such is My decree."

tween German and Yiddish aren't always so clear. I've heard that around the turn of the century, Orthodox Jews in America, with the backing of Jacob Schiff, decided that America needed a chief rabbi. They brought in Rabbi Jacob Joseph of Vilna. They arranged for the rabbi to speak at the Great Synagogue on Suffolk Street, and since he wanted to impress the German Jews, he decided to speak in German. Nobody understood a word he said. When the German Jewish listeners were asked what he had said, they replied, "I don't know, he spoke Yiddish," and when the East European listeners were asked what he had said, they said, "I don't know, he spoke German."

COMMENTARY

Noble actually spoke during ten sessions. At the first, I forgot to bring my tape recorder. The record of that session consists of my notes, written at home immediately afterward. In retrospect they appear remarkably detailed, and I freely assume they are generally accurate and complete. Since they deal for the most part with Noble's family background and earliest childhood, they are of compelling interest.

In a way the notes are already mine, not Noble's, and many of the qualms about reordering, removal of redundancies and filling in gaps which I am faced with when considering the transcript did not give me pause in "writing up" these notes for the book. I could have chosen in fact *not* to write them up, but to reprint them verbatim, since the clipped, journalistic "objective" tone of my original notes contrasts so well with the main narrative, and since they seemed a fair representation of ethnographers' and oral historians' interview notes before tape recordings were widely used. Yet to leave it at that would betray Noble's own wish to communicate his experience to an audience that grew up in another world. Unlike the rest of the book, then, this brief chapter is cast in the "as told to" genre of would-be autobiography.

Also unlike the rest of the book, in this first session Noble was largely responding to questions Charles Nydorf and I asked. The material lacks the structured, cross-referential quality of the other interviews, and thus I present it here without the thematic analysis which follows the rest of the chapters. Nevertheless, the themes of cultural diversity among Jews, the politics of language use, social change and loss of coherence in response to dramatically altered circumstances—themes which inform the entire account—are already present in this fragmentary record of Noble's childhood.

2

The Great War in Sanok

JB: If you have the patience, I'd like to remain in Sanok for this hour.

SN: Yes, yes.

JB: We spoke about legends and so forth, but we actually didn't talk about lifeways.

SN: We stopped with the war years. I told you up to the war years. I mentioned that there was a special commission of heads of households, who tested schoolchildren.

JB: Do you remember the name now, or not?

SN: No, I can't remember. I'll remember, I'll tell you . . . because the son of the *moyre roe*[1] is a librarian in the Seminary.

---

1. In East European Jewish communities, the *moyre roe* was responsible for deciding questions of Jewish ritual law.

Unfortunately he is very, very ill. He has cancer. And I must run to ask him, because if he dies, God forbid, no one will know. He will probably remember what the commission was called. He is younger than me, but . . . he was just a small child then, but . . .

JB: Also a heder boy.

SN: No, he was still a small child.

In our conversation, we got as far as the war years. For you this will be terribly important: in those years, the first war years, traditional Jewish life was thoroughly disrupted. And precisely during the war. And I will tell you why. Understand: at that time I didn't understand this at all. Now I understand it. It was like this: First of all, the war itself took away fathers, and sons— young men. That itself somewhat demoralized the community. A general demoralization. It demoralized Jews, it demoralized Gentiles as well, you understand.

In addition it was like this: Traditional life suffered from two very strong factors which demoralized Jewish life. I will only speak of Sanok, but it was probably the same in other cities as well. When the Russian Army occupied our region—the eastern part of Galicia—most people in Sanok escaped toward Western Austria—to Vienna, to Prague, to Brünn, and other western areas. In Vienna it was impossible to walk around with long, curly sidelocks, nor in a *kapote*,[2] with—you know, the buttons,[3] they couldn't wear that either. Well, when they returned later, let's say three years or two years later, they returned from Vienna with modern clothes. And strange—those who returned from Vienna didn't put their old clothes back on. They returned from

2. Long black overgarment worn by traditionalist Hasidim.
3. Strictly Orthodox and traditionalist European Jewish males wore coats with buttons on the left, the reverse of the secular convention, in order to observe the precept of maintaining a "visible difference" between Jewish and Gentile dress.

Vienna without the sidelocks, and they continued without side-locks. They had gotten used to it. The same with women. In our town before the war there was nothing but *sheytlekh*—no women went—you know what a sheytl[4] is?

JB, CN: Yes, yes.

SN: In Vienna they hadn't worn sheytlekh. First of all, there was no place to buy a sheytl. You understand. When they came back, they wore their own hair. When they came back, they didn't shave their heads again. They went out without sheytlekh.

For instance, *shtraymlekh*[5] became rare. Why? In Vienna they hadn't worn any shtraymlekh in the street, as in Sanok. Nor in Prague. In Vienna they had worn black hats.

That was one factor in the demoralization of the structure of Jewish life. In addition, there was a true moral problem as well. There were no young men in town, but there were girls.

JB: The young men went into the army.

SN: Of course! They were taken into the army from the age of eighteen. So those in the city were boys like me—there were a good number of us—or old men. There were grandfathers and grandchildren, but very few fathers.

But there were girls, many young girls. And there were soldiers as well. Among the soldiers there were various—you know what a soldier is. Amoral, not so amoral . . . and there came about, I remember, one incident. A girl drowned herself. She jumped into a well. Later they drew her out. And I couldn't understand it. I asked my mother: "Mama, why did that girl go and throw herself into the well?"

4. A wig, here used to cover a married woman's head for purposes of modesty.
5. Fur-fringed hat worn by Hasidic men on Sabbath and holidays.

She said to me: *"Zi hot zikh banarisht."*
I said: *"Zi hot zikh banarisht?"*

JB: She went crazy?

SN: No, no. She committed a folly, she got raped. I said, "Mama, what does that mean—*zi hot zikh banarisht?*"

"Don't ask any questions! You won't understand it anyway, a baby . . ." I was ten or eleven years old. Was my mother going to tell me the girl had gotten pregnant? When a girl in Sanok got pregnant, it was a tragedy for her family, and she knew it was her fault. In a good family. This was the result of the war years, it wasn't normal.

In addition many people from Sanok remained in Vienna, in Prague and in Brünn at that time. People came from other cities into Sanok. Wherever there's a new population, morality is always disrupted somewhat. In an established community, everybody knows—I know Yoynesn, Yoynesn knows me, and Yoynesn knows Shimen and Shimen knows me . . . People are careful.

In a strange city, why did I have to be careful? *"Careful? Cheer up, old bird. Nobody knows me around here."* Strange people came, and they didn't behave according to the standards of Sanok. For example, I remember that it was the custom to play *kvitlekh* on Hanukkah—do you know what *kvitlekh* are? Hasidic cards, which we made ourselves. Cards with beautiful women Hasidim wouldn't hold in their hands. But on Hanukkah it's a *mitzvah* to play *kvitlekh*. And I used to go, let's say in the evening, to see, to watch them playing *kvitlekh*. Suddenly I see—no players. No players! It was over. Those who used to play *kvitlekh* weren't interested anymore. And nobody else came—as I said, there were very, very few young people. We played with other things—we played with a *dreydl*,[6] but we didn't play with *kvitlekh*

---

6. A four-sided top played with on Hanukkah.

anymore. And the women who came back wore slightly shorter dresses than had been the custom with us, they were more modern already, and . . . I remember—it's a silly thing—I remember that many women came back, young girls, with pince-nez. That was a sign of big-city culture, of emancipation, they had liberated themselves with the pince-nez.

That's how it was throughout the war years. In the year 1916 the hunger began; food began to be a serious problem. The city was extremely impoverished. The peasants, who still had a bit of potatoes or some other kind of vegetables, or a bit of eggs, milk or butter—the peasants got smart. They came and said they didn't want to sell anything for money. They only wanted to barter. People exchanged things: "What do you want?" They wanted to see what the Jews had.

I remember for example that in 1916 my mother sold my father's shtrayml. She sold it to a baker, a Jewish baker, for ten loaves of bread. You can understand how much bread cost—it was an expensive shtrayml. My father was still a young man, the shtrayml was almost completely new. It was made out of sable, very good. But my mother saw that before we died of hunger . . . She went to the cellar, to the baker, and she said to him, "How much will you give me?"

He said, "Give me the shtrayml." She gave him the shtrayml, and he gave her ten loaves of bread. That is—each week he gave her a loaf. Ten weeks he did it—my mother went to him and he gave her a loaf of bread.

The demoralization grew greater from day to day, despite the appeals of the rabbis. I was studying with a melamed at that time, Pinyele Melamed. I'll never forget him. But this Pinyele Melamed—there was a terrible inflation. He couldn't live on the tuition. Pinyele Melamed began to swindle a bit. He left the children in heder and went to trade at the market. He sold things that the Gentiles were very much in need of and couldn't obtain—they were very eager for sugar; salt, there was a shortage; kerosene—not for automobiles but for lamps; and other things. At one point there was even a shortage of matches. So this Pinyele went out trading at the market. Actually he would tell us, "Read it over, children, read it over." But you know how children are—we ourselves went out, and we didn't just play, various things, we worked a bit . . .

This Pinyele was in general a *genarnik*—someone who fools others, a cheat. We used to study in the evening. Since there was no kerosene, he told each boy to bring a candle. I brought a candle, and this is what happened: He set up all the candles right next to him. I was on the other side. I saw badly, and I had to read—we were learning the Five Books with Rashi's commentary. I strained my eyes very badly, because I couldn't read it, and probably I never had very good eyes. My eyes became red and swollen. I remember it very, very well, I'll never forget it. Do you know—I don't know if you've ever experienced this—a candle gives off a meager light. It was a long table, Pinyele sat here and I sat at the other end.

So my eyes grew worse and worse. I came home and I complained, "Mother, I can't see. There's very little light in the heder, and I have to read the Bible with Rashi." You know what Rashi looks like, you had the experience a few months ago.[7]

But my mother said, "Go. Nevertheless, go."

Once he said to me, "Shloyme—read."

I said, "Rebbe,[8] I can't."

"What's the matter?"

"Look at my eyes."

He came up to me, took a look. "Oh, it's nothing." He went

7. During the semester prior to the recording of these tapes, Noble presented a seminar on the traditional Yiddish glosses on the Bible known as *khumesh-taytsh*. In that seminar he also taught the students how to read what is called "Rashi script," named after the great Bible and Talmud scholar whose commentaries are usually printed in the script. Most of the *khumesh-taytsh* texts are also printed in Rashi script.

8. This term is commonly used in Yiddish to address a teacher as well as a Hasidic leader.

off, to a bookcase. He took out a book, blew the dust off, looked inside and said, "Aha." It was a book of remedies. Maybe it was three hundred or four hundred years old, who knows? If only we had it here now! And he said to me—"Now I know what to do."

CN: Was it *Sefer refues?*[9]

SN: No, no. It was much earlier than that. And this was in Hebrew, the Holy Tongue. *Sefer refues* is in Yiddish.

And he went into the kitchen.

His wife came out with a piece of cold veal, and said to me, "Look in the book of remedies. This is the best remedy—putting on veal."

He took the veal, cut it, and put small pieces on both of my eyes and said, "Today you don't have to read. Just sit and listen." I sat and listened.

I came home, and my eyes were terribly red and bloody. My mother said to me, "What happened?"

I answered her, "Mama, I complained to Pinyele that I couldn't see. And he said, 'Oh, I know the cure.' He put two pieces of meat on my eyes." I went to sleep; I was tired.

In the morning I woke up and shouted, "Mama, mama, I'm blind. I can't open my eyes."

Of course, my mother grabbed me. There weren't any doctors there. With the doctors it was like this: the young doctors were in the army. We went to the *feldsher*, the traditional healer. What did the healer know? Nevertheless he knew that it was wrong to place meat over the eyes. He was a Christian—Rober was his name—not a bad man. Rober took a look and said, "Well, what happened? Tell me the truth."

My mother stood nearby and signaled to me, "Shh! Don't tell

9. *Sefer refues* simply means, "Book of Remedies." There are at least three volumes with this title, and it is difficult to know which one is meant here.

him anything at all about Pinyele." Because, you understand, if I had said why Pinyele had placed the pieces of meat over my eyes, the healer—he was a Christian—would have said, "Oh, I'll show him, practicing medicine without a license."

So my mother ordered me not to say anything, and I didn't say a thing: "I don't know, I don't know."

So he prescribed the following remedy, which I remember as if it were today: "Take a piece of bread or cotton, dip it in warm milk and place it over the eyes." The question was where to get milk during the war years. My mother went to visit a woman who had a brother in a village not far away, and asked the woman to simply give her a drop of milk for soaking, and that helped.

But we couldn't stay in the city. There just wasn't anything to eat. Sometimes potatoes appeared. And then it was possible to buy two or three pounds of potatoes. We had potatoes for breakfast, at lunch and for supper. There were other things that we had three times a day, day after day. My mother had a sister in a village, twenty kilometers from the city, not far. My mother decided—first of all, I'm the oldest child, in addition to me there was a brother and a sister—my mother said, "You know what, my children. You know that we don't have anything to eat. Go away, at least you'll have something to eat, go to your aunt in the village." My grandfather was also staying with that aunt.

So I went to the village. And *I had it very, very good there.* First of all we had food. There was bread, fruit, various vegetables, cabbage, enough potatoes. I stayed in the village.

The problem with the village was that I had no Jewish friends. And you know what a child who has no Jewish friends does. I became friendly with Ukrainians—the whole village was Ukrainian. I became friendly with Ukrainian boys, and I became altogether Ukrainized. I began speaking Ukrainian, and that was— *that was my undoing.* They taught me various things that a city boy didn't know. They taught me to catch fish, how to ride a horse. They taught me all these things. They also taught me how to catch birds. But the birds were killed. We didn't catch them live. You took a long board, and rested it on a piece of wood. We spread out a bit of grain under the board. And we tied a piece of string to the piece of wood that held the board. The birds didn't see the string. When the birds saw grain, they came running to eat it. We would tug on the string—we were hidden behind a tree—and when we pulled the string, what happened? The board fell, and we had dead birds. We did it for the meat. There wasn't much—an *ounce* or two—nevertheless it was something good to have meat to eat.

And the Gentile boys taught me other similar things. And I liked them very much. They never did anything bad to me, they included me in all their play, wherever they went they took me along. I remember one time—they used to graze the horses day and night. With the horses it was like this: The horses that worked by day—plowing, or other fieldwork—were combed at night and grazed all night. One time they took me along, and I sat with them all night. And what did we do? They sang sad Ukrainian songs, and we made a fire. We took potatoes along and we threw them into the fire and roasted and ate them. There was never—they knew that I was a Jew, they even reminded me, they had learned that they had to remind me to recite a blessing. They knew that I couldn't eat without reciting a blessing. And they knew that I only ate with a hat on my head. On the contrary, it was entirely natural: "He's a *Zhid*[10]—and he has his ways, quite strange ways actually, but we're different." On the contrary: they liked me very much and never did me any harm.

As I said, I became quite Ukrainized. I spoke the Ukrainian language with them constantly. And that was my problem. One

10. Slavic term for Jew, usually derogatory.

Friday before a special Sabbath — it was the first day of the Jewish month, as well — my grandfather said to me, "Well, in honor of the Sabbath, we'll go catch some fish."

I said, "Grandfather, I'm very good at catching fish." And we went fishing. I can't say exactly how many I caught, but my luck just stayed with me the whole time. I caught many, many fish. I became very, very excited, and I forgot that I was with my grandfather. We were sitting in a boat, you understand, and we had a net. We'd toss the net in, and we'd bang on the water with a long piece of wood. The fish came out, and we grabbed them in the net. I caught quite a lot, and became excited, and shouted: *"Jesu! Shtotu ryb!"* In Ukrainian. I'd heard the Ukrainians, they would say that. You know what "Jesu" means. "Jesus! Look how many fish we caught! A hundred!"

My grandfather grew sad. He didn't say anything, not a word. He said, "Nu, enough. We won't catch any more fish." It was Friday afternoon. We came home. My aunt cooked the fish we'd caught. My grandfather didn't speak to me the whole day, didn't say a thing to me that Friday night. And on Saturday he didn't say a word to me the whole day. And I understood that something — *something's brewing.* The next day, very early, my grandfather said to me, "Say your prayers."

I was surprised: Why is he telling me to pray so early? He said, "We're returning to Sanok."

I started protesting, but —

"You won't stay in the village any longer, because if you stay in the village, you'll become, God forbid, a — what?

JB: "A Goy."

SN: A Goy. He didn't want to say it. But with his "you'll become, God forbid" — I already understood what. If he meant I'd become a rabbi, he wouldn't have said "God forbid."

I cried, I begged for mercy, I said "Grandfather, I won't hang around with the Gentile boys any longer." He understood that there weren't any other Jewish boys with whom I could be friendly. Children don't sit by themselves. Anyway they used to come, they'd come into the house and take me out, show me various things.

I came back into town, and incidentally, my grandfather returned to town with me. And he said, "Well—let's go see if we can find a proper melamed."

My grandfather said to me, "In a year you'll be a Jew—in a year you'll be a Bar Mitzvah boy—and you know such worthless things." He placed me in a heder with a melamed. His name was Menashele Melamed. I learned Gemore.

JB: And was that when your grandfather established the society to examine the children in their studies?

SN: To examine them, no. That was earlier, before I went off to the countryside. When they examined the children I was learning only Bible with Rashi. I wasn't learning Gemore yet.

JB: Were you ever in a yeshiva?

SN: Here in New York.

JB: I'm interested in the domestic lifeways. A day in Sanok.

SN: We got up in the morning, poured water on our hands— you know what that means—*neglvaser*. We'd say *moyde ani*, you know what that means, don't you? *Moyde ani lifonekho melekh khay vekayam,*[11] and so forth. Begin praying. I'd have the prayer-book in my hand, and sometimes I'd look into the kitchen. My

11. This is the beginning of the standard prayer upon awakening. It expresses thanks to God for guarding the individual's soul during the night.

grandfather would look to see if I was really looking at the prayerbook, or if I was looking out at the street. You know, sometimes I'd look out at the street. Sometimes I'd see a goat, or a dog would be running along, one that I didn't know. My mother heard that it was quiet, I wasn't saying anything, she'd say, "Listen, what are you doing there?" Although I did pray, too.

I'd go and wash before eating, recite a blessing, and she'd give me whatever there was to eat. It was during the war, and there was very little to eat. When I'd finished eating, I'd go into heder. Like all heder children, I studied a lot and played a bit also.

JB: How many children were there in the heder?

SN: How many children? I'll tell you in a minute. This was a Bible with Rashi heder. This was Pinyele Melamed's class. There were about thirty children in the class.

JB: Really? It was a big heder, no?

SN: Yes—but all in one class. They all learned the same thing.

JB: In what room was it, in what building?

SN: It was in the teacher's bedroom. In the middle there was a long table with two long benches on both sides of the table, and the teacher sat at one end with his whip in his hand—you know what a *kantshik* is—a cat-o'-nine-tails. And he simply paid attention to make sure that the children were looking into the Bible, not at the wall or the window.

But he wasn't a bad melamed, this Pinyele. Until he began cheating during the war, and then it was bad. He used to go out into the street and peddle. With matches, various small items, needles, various things the peasants needed, pins.

Everybody peddled. Everybody peddled at that time.

So when I came back later—I was in the village for about two years all told—my grandfather came back with me. One incident that I almost forgot, and now that I've started talking . . . In heder there was a game. After all, we sat in the heder all day. Until quite late in the evening. Well, it was impossible to study the whole time. So we played a bit as well.

There was no floor in the heder. So we children dug out a little depression in the middle, and we used to play with buttons. You'd give it a push, and whoever got his into the depression was the winner. And it was an established game.

But this is how things were: I was virtually the youngest boy in the heder. I was about ten or eleven. There were older boys as well. It was a question of ability. Anybody who was less capable would still be in a class of Bible with Rashi at age thirteen or so. He wouldn't be in a Gemore class yet.

And now I see boys have really different ideas about life. I remember it was like this—you're students of sociology, you know that every group of students creates their own mores. It was accepted among the students that when boys play buttons, and one has lost all his buttons, he had the right to say, "Give me a *ptshitshenik.*" That means, let me play one round for free. And he was given it. It was thus accepted. *These were the mores of the trade.* When a boy lost all the buttons he had, we took buttons—from old clothes, even from my own clothes—I cut buttons off, and told my mother I'd lost them.

Now you'll have to excuse me, I'm going to tell you something that's not so pretty. But I didn't understand it then. It was accepted that when a student lost, he'd say, "Give me a *ptshitshenik.*" That's a Polish word, it means—how would you say it in English, it means "*Give me a break,*" you know, "*Let me play one game.*" Without putting anything into the pot. We had to put a button into the depression. And the one who had lost all his buttons was allowed to play without putting a button in. But only once. If he had bad luck and lost that time too, the custom was to sing to him: *"Tanin veodom vekhayes re'emim."*[12] That meant—"a fish, and a person, and a bison."

And my grandfather always paid close attention—as soon as I would come home, he'd ask me what I'd learned in heder. I told him, "We learned such and such and such . . ."

And he'd say, "Good, good, good."

"We played a bit . . ."

One time I was sitting, and this *"Tanin veodom vekhayes re'-emim"* is in the songs for Friday night: *"Tanin veodom vekhayes re'emim/ ki biyo adonoy tsur olamim."* I don't know how that came to us children. Someone came up with this witticism: *"Tanin veodom vekhayes re'emim/ az me hot nit kayn gelt, shpilt men mitn kleynem."*[13] That's how the rhyme went. I didn't understand at all what "the little thing" was, what it meant. So once I was sitting quite naively, and I said it to myself, and I remembered that once a boy had lost all his buttons, and they had sung at him, *"Tanin veodom vekhayes re'emim/ az me hot nit kayn kneplekh, shpilt men mitn kleynem."*

My grandfather heard. He came up to me, frightened. He asked me, "Where did you hear that?"

I said, "I learned it."

"Where did you hear it?"

"In heder."

"From whom?"

"From the boys, the boys. Everybody sings it." I started telling him, "You see, Grandfather, it's like this. When you lose all your buttons . . ." He didn't know what that was, that when we played with buttons there was a depression we aimed the buttons at. So I explained to him that when a boy had bad luck and lost all his buttons, he asked for a free chance. And when he lost

12. This is a line of a Sabbath hymn called *Menukhe vesimkhe* ("Rest and Joy").

13. "If you don't have any money/you play with the little thing"—here evidently a euphemism for the penis.

again, that's when the boys sang this song. And they'd say, "You don't play anymore. You go outside when we play."

"Really?" he said. "That's what they teach you in heder?"

I said, "No. Just from the children, not from the teacher."

My grandfather immediately took me by the hand, and said, "Come. We're going to the heder." And my grandfather let out his anger at Pinyele the teacher: "You don't attend to the children. So! This is a melamed? You don't hear what they do, what they say? They say crude things among themselves, and you pretend you don't hear?"

He immediately took me out of the heder. I never spent another hour in that heder. And he sent me to another heder.

The other heder was Menashele's. And I learned Gemore with Menashele. Menashele was on a higher level. Did I ever go over with you the gradations? Alphabet heder, half-syllable heder, do you know what that is—"What's this—a *komets*;[14] what's this—a *pasek*; what's this—a *tsere*; what's this above—an *aleph*; and what's underneath the *aleph*—a *komets*." First the vowels were learned by heart, and then they were put together. "What's this—an *aleph*. What's underneath the *aleph*—a *komets*. What does that make—*aw*. What's this—a *beyz*. What's under the *beyz*—a *pasek*. What does that make— *ba*." I don't know how we stood this. It went on for hours, "*baw, ba, be*."

JB: And there was a separate heder for that?

SN: Yes, yes. But for only one semester. Then we went on to whole syllables, *baw, ba, be*, and then we read the prayerbook, and then we began Bible. The higher level was Bible with Rashi. And the level beyond that was Gemore.

We learned Gemore with Menashele. But here you'll have

14. *Komets, tsere* and *pasek* are all Hebrew vowel markings; *aleph* is the first letter of the Hebrew alphabet.

some difficulty, and I'll have to explain it, because it has to do with Hebrew grammar. I remember that we were learning a tractate of the Gemore called Khulin.[15] In this tractate there is a passage called "meat and milk." And the Mishnah[16] begins: "*Halev kore umotsi es domo.*" The heart: since there is blood in the heart, you have to cut the heart and let the blood out. (You know that it was forbidden to eat blood.) "*Hakhal*"—that is the udder—"*kore umotsi es*"—and the scholars, among us they said "*khelbo*," which is from "*kheylev*," which means fat. But in fact it should be read "*khalovo.*" It should be read "*khalovo,*" and the scholars said "*khelbo.*" Now Menashele was a bit of a *maskil.*[17] And he knew enough grammar to know that you shouldn't say "*khelbo,*" but rather "*khalovo.*" "*Khalovo*" means "its milk." "*Hakhal*"—the udder—"*kore*"—is cut—"*umotsi es khalovo*"—and the milk is taken out. You know that meat and milk are forbidden to be eaten together.

So every day I came home and my grandfather asked me. My grandfather had bad eyes, he couldn't read. But he remembered. And I told him, and he remembered by heart. I said to him, "*Halev kore umotsi es domoy; hakhal kore umotsi es khalovo.*" I said, "*khalovo.*"

He said, "What did you say? What did you say? Let me hear it again."

I repeated, "*khalovo.*"

"Ah, *khalovo.*" My grandfather began stroking his beard, this way and that way. "So. So. *Khalovo.*" He was talking to himself, a monologue. "Seems to me it's actually correct. According to the *Shaarey toyre*"—a book of grammar written in the eighteenth

15. A Talmudic tractate which deals with questions of *kashrut*. The passage in question begins on folio 109a.

16. The Mishnah is the earlier of the two redacted texts which comprise the Talmud; "Gemore," commonly used in Yiddish to indicate the entire Talmud, more particularly refers to the portions redacted later, which themselves are structured as commentary on the Mishnah.

17. A follower of the Haskalah, the Jewish Enlightenment.

century by Reb Zalmen Hanau, from Germany, near Frankfurt-am-Main—Reb Zalmen wrote *Shaarey toyre*, and there he says indeed that we should read this, *khalovo*. "Is that correct?" my grandfather said to himself. And he repeated again: "*Halev kore umotsi es domoy; hakhal kore umotsi es khalovo.*"

"Nevertheless," he said, "the man's a grammarian. *Shema mino*—we learn from this—that he looks at books of grammar. And if he looks at books of grammar, he's a maskil!"

You know, a pious Jew wouldn't study grammar. And so my grandfather took me out of Menashele's heder.

But I must tell you—the sensibility of these Jews, to catch something like that. Years later, perhaps a week before I left for America—I was already almost fifteen years old—I went past Menashele's heder. It was known in town that I too was a maskil, the *maskilim* considered me as one of their comrades. He knew me since I had spent some time studying with him. He ran out: "Shloymele, Shloymele, come, I want to show you something. Come, Shloymele."

I went in, and he looked around. There was no one there; it was very late, after heder. He looked around, and he looked out the window, and he went to the bed and from underneath the straw mattress he pulled out a book. Guess what the book was?

CN: Goethe.

SN: No, no, even worse. Mendelssohn's *Biur*.[18] The first time in my life I had seen it before my eyes. Oh, if they had known about it in Sanok—not only his heder, they would have burned him as well! And you see that my grandfather somehow sensed

18. Moses Mendelssohn (1729–1786) was a German Jewish intellectual who was among the founders of the Haskalah, the Jewish Enlightenment. The *Biur*, his German translation and commentary on the Bible, was considered anathema by militantly traditionalist Jews.

this. I already studied grammar on my own by then. I've told you that I was a member at that time of Hashomer Hatsair.[19]

JB: Beginning at what age, what year?

SN: From 1917 on. I was twelve years old at that time. In 1917 Shalom Spiegel[20] came—you know who he is?

CN: Yes, the Hebraist.

SN: Shalom Spiegel. He came to our town. He was the founder of Hashomer Hatsair. He came to town to recruit children for the organization.

CN: How old was he?

SN: I'll tell you in a second . . . In 1917 Shalom Spiegel was eighteen years old. A tall young man, blond, and I began to read and to read, and I was in Hashomer Hatsair. One Sabbath we were walking, and Shalom Spiegel sat, and there was an open-air cafe in Sanok. And he sat there drinking coffee.

And my grandfather said to me, "It seems to me that's your . . . *shomrot?*" He didn't know the difference, *shomrot, shomeret.* "What's he doing there? Is that one of your comrades?"

I said, "I don't know. Maybe yes, but I don't know . . ."

He said, "Oh, yes, it's him. Ohhhh . . . to that Jewish sinner you'll go? No, you won't go."

But in any case he went away very shortly afterward. I wept and complained to my mother, but they wouldn't let me go to

19. The Jewish scouting organization, which later adopted Marxist principles and served as the origin of the left Zionist Israeli political party Mapam.
20. Shalom Spiegel (1899–1984) became a Jewish scholar and served for many years on the faculty of the Jewish Theological Seminary in New York.

Hashomer Hatsair. But I kept going, at the same time as I went to heder.

And so my Bar Mitzvah approached. The Bar Mitzvah was nothing, nothing. There was no food to give anybody. My mother wept. We were supposed to give something to eat to everybody, but what could we do when there wasn't a piece of bread around? There was absolutely nothing at all. I said, "Nu, there'll be something." I went off to pray, I put on my *tefillin*,[21] and my grandfather recited the blessing which my father was supposed to make—my grandfather made it *bimkom tate*, in my father's stead. And so it went, until the war ended in 1918, and my father came home. Things went back to normal, more or less. But Jewish life had been thoroughly shaken.

21. Small leather boxes containing Scripture, worn on the head and arm by Orthodox men while praying.

COMMENTARY

This chapter—the record of the first interview that was actually taped—begins in interview format. Using a cultural historian as my native informant and storyteller, I was able to use the professional terminology, as when I attempt to prompt Noble: "I'm interested in the domestic lifeways. A day in Sanok." Although Noble responds to this request, his response actually forms a brief digression between two long monologues. Noble doesn't continue his formal, summary description of a typical day past breakfast. At this point, I was still looking for patterns; Noble was already telling stories.

Of course, Noble was well aware of his audience, and used the setting to help structure his stories. A sharp example of this occurs when, in order to illustrate the personal interaction in established communities, Noble uses the first-person pronoun, my name and the name "Shimen"—the Talmudic equivalent of John Doe—"In an established community, everybody knows—I know Yoynesn, Yoynesn knows me, and Yoynesn knows Shimen and Shimen knows me . . ." This kind of inclusion constitutes a kind of dialogic ethnography which is to a great extent controlled by the "informant"—whom we should really call the storyteller. The collector of the story, rather than a puppeteer pulling strings, becomes instead a prop for the storyteller.

As I first learned from Barbara Myerhoff's wonderful book *Number Our Days*,[22] elderly people use a storytelling opportunity to create themselves in retrospect. When Noble tells us, toward the beginning of this chapter, "At that time I didn't understand this at all. Now I understand it," he reminds us that he is now reflecting, analyzing, not merely reporting what was in his mind at the time. There is a hint that he may be getting the chance to rework memories that have been dormant for years.

As an ironic counterpoint to Walter Benjamin's suggestion that World War I shattered the possibilities of storytelling, Noble offers several brief vignettes which illuminate that very break. The

22. New York: Simon & Schuster, 1976.

change is described first and foremost as the loss of material cultural forms, under the pressure of sheer want or of a forced confrontation with urban modernity. Noble's mother exchanged the Hasidic fur hat belonging to his father—who was away serving in the Austrian Army—for a ten-weeks supply of bread. People lost interest in the traditional game of cards at Hanukkah. Women who had been in Vienna as refugees stopped wearing modest wigs when the war ended. The anomie of refugee life, which prompted these abandonments, is expressed by a sentence in which Noble suddenly switches to English: *"Careful? Cheer up, old bird. Nobody knows me around here."*

Tricksters will always see such dislocations as opportunities, however. The hunger in Sanok forces Noble and his grandfather into the countryside, among Ukrainian boys, and as he says in English, *"I had it very, very good there."* Although Noble stresses that the Ukrainian boys helped him to maintain his Jewish customs, he does not remark on one way in which he obviously failed to observe Jewish law: the small birds which he ate along with the other boys clearly were not killed according to the rules of kashrut. He continues: "I began speaking Ukrainian, and that was—[English] *that was my undoing.*" One could claim that at that moment, Noble couldn't think of a way to say "That was my undoing" in Yiddish. Nevertheless, since the phrase reflects back on a reference to the cultural danger of non-Jewish languages, a series of ironic commentaries is implied: His childhood contact with Ukrainian village boys was his "undoing" because it dissolved his fear and mistrust of Gentiles; his childhood use of Ukrainian led to his adult use of English in the world of secular scholarship; just as he was "undone" by Ukrainian, so Charles and I are "undone" since birth in English, our native language, and must be "remade" through the Yiddish which he, among others, teaches us. Yet Noble never became a penitent or a purist: even here, he insists twice that "on the contrary"—that is, to any assumptions that the Ukrainian boys would have been anti-Semitic—they treated him very well and helped him maintain his Jewish ways. This, in contrast to the episode with the Cossacks recounted in Chapter 1, is an early positive experience of being Jewish and "different."

For all his love of the traditional Jewish world, Noble makes it clear that there was a good deal worth escaping. His frightful temporary brush with blindness, along with his teacher's callous ignorance, are captured in the image of a medical book which was so outdated that the teacher had to "blow the dust off" before he could use it. The poignant empathy with the suffering of the child Noble had been is combined with a scholar's retrospective passion for the obsolete knowledge which helped cause that suffering: "If only we had it here now!"

Noble's early sensitivity toward language—suggested in the first chapter, when he reports being moved by the very sound of the language of the Hallel prayer—is matched by an impatience with rote repetition. His bafflement at young boys' survival of the numbing heder routine, "*baw, ba, be* for hours" is consistent with his admission that he preferred looking out the window to reciting his morning prayers. This criticism is a staple of Yiddish secularist culture, echoed in the sentimental folksong *Afn pripetshik*: "Say it again, and yes, once again: *komets aleph, aw*." Here as well there may be a hint at the origin for his preference of pedagogic storytelling over rote repetition.

Yet not every heder was the same, nor was every melamed the same. Pinyele was ignorant of medical matters and negligent of the children. They indulged the resulting freedom to display the innate subversiveness of children, mixing sacred hymns with vulgarity in the macaronic couplet "*Tanin veodom vekhayes re'emim/ az me hot nit kayn kneplekh, shpilt men mitn kleynem.*" Young Shlomo and the other children were probably unaware of it, but the second line of the song refers explicitly to the Almighty. Hence his grandfather's shocked reaction to the substitution of a Yiddish euphemism for the penis reveals not simple prudery, but extreme caution against even unwitting blasphemy.

Menashele, on the other hand, simply knew too much, as evidenced by his contextually correct reading *khalovo*—"its milk"—rather than *khelbo*—"its fat." Even though there was an earlier rabbinic authority for this reading, the taint of secular grammar was sufficiently damning, as far as Noble's grandfather was concerned.

Noble clearly respects his grandfather's correct deduction that this correction indicated Menashele's lack of traditional piety—a kind of ethnography against Enlightenment. On the other hand, the result was that the grandfather was forced to pull Shlomo out of two heders, another indication of the crisis of traditional life in wartime.

Several themes which help illustrate Noble's scholarly esthetic are revealed here. First, the recognition that the "human sciences" had a place in the traditional religious world as well, that belief and critique sometimes share common ground. Second, the awareness that a struggle for predominance when belief and critique do appear in contradiction is a dynamic present in every culture. Third, the acceptance that belief often wins out in that struggle, and that a student of culture must give belief the chance to speak.

Perhaps the most elegant bit of linguistic play in the entire series of interviews comes during Noble's description of his Bar Mitzvah. With his father away in the army, his grandfather had to recite the father's blessing *bimkom tate*—in his father's stead. In synagogue ritual, the word *"bimkom"* almost inevitably is followed by *"levi,"* since it is used when a Kohen recites the second blessing over the Torah reading in the place of an absent Levi. There are three elements to this phrase of Noble's, then. First, the reference to substitution for the party who by rights should fill a ritual function. Second, the switch in lexical category—"grandfather" in place of "father," rather than *"kohen"* in place of *"levi."* Third, the switch in language—the Yiddish *"tate"* in place of the Hebrew *"levi."* The enormity of the disruption is matched by the resilience of the cultural idiom in which it is expressed.

3

A Sort of Flowering, but No Future

SN: There was a political shift after the war: Austria fell apart, and in its place there were Poland, Czechoslovakia, Yugoslavia and the other states, and we became part of Poland. Galicia became part of Poland, and it became entirely different. The border to Great Poland opened up, and Hasidim from Poland wearing their—you know, they came to us with the Polish—you know Polish Hasidim wear *kashketelekh*,[1] we used to call them. Sometime I'll show you a picture of it. We have pictures of it here. And when they came from Poland we saw that in Poland they didn't wear shtraymlekh, and in general, life grew less and less traditional all the time. For example, when my father came back, he didn't have a shtrayml. And my mother told him, "Quite simply, in order to keep the children alive. I got ten loaves of bread for it."

He said, "Very well, but what shall we do?" And all the rest, practically everyone else who didn't have a shtrayml—they wore hats.

1. A type of cap.

JB: Did people wear shtraymlekh every day before then?

SN: No! Only on the Sabbath and holidays.

I remember this, for example: My father didn't have a shtrayml, and my aunt—my father's sister—not the one from the village, but a different one, from a nearby town, a town called Baligrod. Who comes from Baligrod—Sidney Morgenbesser[2] comes from Baligrod. Sidney Morgenbesser said to me once that no one remembers that such a shtetl exists. I said, "Listen, what do you mean no one remembers? My grandfather was the *dayan* in that town. Of course I remember it."

When my father came home, my aunt married off a son. Of course, my father, her only brother, went to the wedding. But my father didn't have a shtrayml. My aunt began to cry, "You're going to go without a shtrayml, like a *daytsh*?" You know what a *daytsh* is?

JB: Yeah, yeah, yeah.

SN: A maskil. In short, my father said, "Listen, Shprintse—my aunt's name was Shprintse—what can I do? I have no money to buy things. I came home from the war. I have no means of livelihood, I can't even buy bread."

In short, Jews are resourceful. A Jew who wasn't going to the wedding loaned my father his shtrayml, and my father went. All shtraymlekh fit. One size fits all.

And then there began another problem: anti-Semitism in Poland increased greatly. In Poland there arose—

JB: Already!

2. Professor of Philosophy at Columbia University.

SN: Immediately after the war, anti-Semitism increased greatly. Anti-Semitism immediately increased. The pogroms—probably you've heard about the pogroms in Poland then, in 1918, 1919.

We personally didn't suffer from any pogroms, but my father said, "I'm afraid that there's no hope here. There's no future here for Jews." And all the same, Jews didn't submit—Jews fought back fiercely, defended synagogues . . .

And it was very strange, there was a kind of flowering of Jewish life. A sort of flowering of Jewish life. There were created, for example, various Jewish organizations. There were Jewish organizations which had been in existence from before. But so many organizations were created, so many organizations. The Zionist organization created an Orthodox branch, the Mizrachi.[3] You've heard of Mizrachi. They were right-wing Zionists, the Mizrachi. Their slogan was the Zionist slogan—you know what the Zionist slogan is, that Zionism strives toward . . . It's the Basel program. You know what the Basel program was?

JB: Yes.

SN: The Mizrachi added to it. They said, "We accept the program that Zionism strives to create a Jewish state in the Land of Israel," and they requested that the words *"al pi Toyres Yisroel"* be added. That means what? "Based on the Jewish Torah."

And a Mizrachi organization was established in our town. The others, further to the left, came and said, "We don't want that. We want to be Zionists, but we want it to be on a socialist basis. We accept the Basel program, and we want to add—just as they added *al pi Toyres Yisroel*, we add 'on a socialist basis.' " That was Poalei Tsion.[4]

Then came an Agudas Yisroel. You know what Agudas Yisroel

3. Founded in 1902; the forerunner of the National Religious Party in Israel.
4. Socialist Zionist movement founded around the turn of the century in Eastern Europe; forerunner of various secular Zionist parties and factions in Israel.

is?[5] And then there was—the Aguda wasn't religious enough for some, and an organization called Shleymey Emuna beYisroel was established, even more religious than the Aguda.[6]

Then there were various *tsiyere*. You know what *tsiyere* means.

JB, CN: No.

SN: No? No?! "Youth." Tsiyere Agudas Yisroel, Tsiyere Mizrachi.

JB: I'd like to ask you to describe Hashomer Hatsair in those years.

SN: Yes. A very good question. Purely a Scouting organization. There were ten commandments that Hashomer kept. Copied precisely from Baden-Powell. You've heard of Baden-Powell?

CN: Yes, the founder of the Boy Scouts.

SN: And they even wore the shirts, did you ever see the shirts? They wore the kerchief, everything was the same—except for what? Yiddish. Only Yiddish. Even the Zionists. I remember—I was ambitious, and I wanted to become a *rosh pluga*, which means a Scout leader. There was a directive from Warsaw, saying that in order to be a leader one had to know Hebrew well. I sat down and I studied, and studied, and studied. I thoroughly learned a grammar text.

5. Agudat Israel, established in 1912 at a conference in Katowice, Upper Silesia, and uniting German, Hungarian and Polish-Lithuanian Orthodox groups. Distant from Zionism but, after 1948, not opposed to the existence of Israel.

6. This reference is unclear. The full name of the Aguda when it was founded was Aguda Shleymey Emuna beYisroel, and scholars I have consulted insist there was never a separate organization to the right of Aguda.

The New Yeshiva

JB: You told us that you would talk about your studies with Reb Dovid Shapiro.

SN: What?

JB: Reb Dovid Shapiro.

SN: No, no. Reb Meir Shapiro.

JB: Reb Meir Shapiro.

SN: Reb Dovid Shapiro was a Hasidic rebbe near us, the Dinever Rebbe they called him. He lived in the shtetl of Dinev. Reb Meir Shapiro came after the war. Just after the first war the town rabbi in Sanok died. An old Jew named Dym, from an old family. And the new town rabbi was Meir Shapiro. He came from a city called Dvornik; in Sanok he was called the Dvorniker Rov. This Reb Meir Shapiro had ambition. He was just burning to do something in Sanok.

(I didn't want to start with this; I wanted to start with another subject.)

But he began thinking about a *yeshiva*.[7] There had never been a yeshiva. There were countless heders; a municipal Talmud Torah;[8] but there was no yeshiva. There were what we called *bes medresh bokherim* and *kloyz bokherim*. You know what *bes medresh bokherim* were? It simply meant that they sat in the study house and studied. These were grown boys already. Let's say fifteen, sixteen—no, older. Even young men sat and studied—*kestnikes*,[9]

7. In this context, "yeshiva" means a religious school for older boys, where they would have primarily studied Talmud.

8. Free education provided by the Jewish community for poor children.

9. *Kest* was the social institution through which newly married young men were supported by their in-laws for a time ranging upward from one year, so that they could increase their rabbinic learning before they began earning a living.

you know what that means? They sat in the study house or synagogue and studied.

So he thought that it was necessary to establish a yeshiva in
Sanok. He was a person with extraordinary organizational abili-
ties, and he succeeded. First of all he approached a rich Jew who
lived not far away from us—Itsik Hertsog was his name—a rich
Jew and a simple Jew, a very simple Jew, didn't know a thing,
and rich. He got a house from this Itsik Hertsog. He had a house
that was big, too big for the yeshiva. Sanok never could have
afforded it . . . But nevertheless he talked and talked to him.
"You know, a man doesn't live forever. And meanwhile, what
good is it doing you," and so forth—and he gave him the house
for the yeshiva.

Nu, how does one organize a yeshiva? How would you have
organized a yeshiva? First he went from melamed to melamed,
and he said, "Give me the better students."

At that time I was learning with a teacher named Levine. I
told you—my grandfather took me away from the teacher who
taught me Gemore according to grammatical principles. "Aha,
someone who's learned in grammar, so he must be a maskil.
And since he's a maskil, he won't do." You know, I found this
phenomenon in the Middle Ages among the Catholic clergy. A
priest sent to the Bishop of Lyons a book he'd written. The
Bishop of Lyons answered, "Dear son of mine. The content of
what you have sent me pleases me very much. However, your
writing is too grammatically correct—a sign that you read Hor-
ace and Virgil and the others." He says, "It would be better if
you knew a little less Latin and devoted yourself to our pious
men. Their grammar is not so fine, but they are pious men, their
yires-shomayim"—you know what yires-shomayim is —

CN: *Fear of God.*

SN: "*Fear of God* is very great among them." And I found this
once among Catholics. And it was the same with Jews. At this

time I was with another melamed, the man was named Levine.
I believe he was from the Ukraine, he wasn't from Sanok.

He walked in—he was such a refined Jew, kept himself so
clean. His beard was combed, and his sidelocks were combed.
Not like our melamdim, their beards were . . . And in that
respect he made quite a good impression. His name was Levine.
And I believe he was later in America. He died in America. I
was studying with him, and we were studying Gitin.[10] I don't
know why we were studying Gitin. I didn't know anything about
marriage, and certainly didn't know how one gets divorced.

He came in the first day, and said, "Children, open the Gemore." There is a Mishnah which is called "Hameyvi get:"[11]
When someone brings a bill of divorce from a vayte medina—that
means a maritime province—tsorekh sheyomar—he has to say—
bifonay nikhtav—I was present when the bill of divorce was written—ubifonay nikhtam. He personally is testifying that the man
who wrote the bill of divorce is the one who is divorcing his
wife.

Levine had a melody for this, and I didn't understand . . .
[sings] "Hameyvi get mimedinas hayam, bim bom bim bom
bom . . ."

I looked into the Gemore; there wasn't any "Bim bom bim
bom bom" there.

"Tsorekh"—and this all rhymed—"tsorekh sheyomar bifonay
nikhtam, bim bom bim bom bom . . ."

And actually I liked this very much. Once I thought to myself: "Listen, it's an insult. He keeps the Gemore with bim bom
bim bom bom for himself, and to me he gives the Gemore without bim bom bim bom bom." Once I stole over and took his
Gemore—"Ekh, there isn't any bim bom bim bom bom here
either!" He was just improvising.

10. The Talmudic tractate dealing with divorce law.
11. Tractate Gitin, Folio 1:A.

And this was his melody: [sings] *"Hameyvi get mimedinas hayam, bim bom bim bom bom."* And we repeated it. You know, children went to heder and repeated the lesson.

So Reb Meir Shapiro came to Levine, and said, "Give me a list of your best children." At that time I had already been Bar Mitzvahed. My name was on the list. And he came to see each one of the children personally. Imagine—the rabbi of the city. He came into the house and he said he wanted me to study in his yeshiva in Sanok, to be among the first students.

I answered him, "Rebbe, I'm a *daytsh*." I had cut off my side-locks, it was after the war, I had already shed Hasidism to some extent, I was in Hashomer Hatsair—"I'm a *daytsh*."

And he said, "A *daytsh* doesn't study Torah in a yeshiva?"

I had no answer to that. I had no answer to that. You know what a *daytsh* is to us—a maskil. So I went to study. I went to study, but not much. I did study with him a bit, but very shortly I went to America.

How to Prevent a Pogrom

SN: And that brings me to what I wanted to start with. I told you that after the war virulent anti-Semitism arose in Poland. You know that in Poland there are anti-Semites. Why? There was competition between Poland and the Ukraine. Now, to the west of Sanok there are Poles, and to the east were only Ukrainians. And there was competition over this province. Ukrainians or Poles. The Poles suspected that the Jews sympathized with the Ukrainians. Somehow they—perhaps it was really true, that the Jews did indeed sympathize with the Ukrainians. I don't know. Incidentally, nationalism grew very strong, both among the Poles and among the Ukrainians. For example, there was a soccer team in our town, a Polish one. And at a certain point a Ukrainian soccer team was created. And I once went to see a match between the two—we actually used the word *match*—and I heard the Ukrainians shouting, "*Strelyai!!*" That's Ukrainian for "Shoot, shoot!" Ukrainian! That had never been.

So a dispute arose between these two, and the Jews were, so to speak, in the middle. So the impression grew among the Poles that the Jews sympathized . . . If something isn't clear, be so good and interrupt me. It doesn't bother me.

JB: We will.

SN: And the anti-Semitism began. You know, the great pogroms, you've certainly heard of the pogrom in Lemberg, the pogrom in Pinsk, when forty-two young people were shot. And people began saying, "Soon it will come to Sanok as well."

My father had been a soldier. In the last years of the war—perhaps for about a year in all—he had been assigned to a construction battalion. You know, they built bridges, various roads, highways . . . Well, you know a Jew, intelligent, my father very quickly became an expert in the problems of road building. For instance, let's say you have to build a road from Sanok to Przemysl. He knew exactly what materials were needed, how many stones—you know the big roads weren't made like the little paths in the village—they were paved with stones. He could figure out exactly how much sand was needed—so that they wouldn't just go ahead and start haphazardly filling wagons with sand. The last year of the war that was his task—building military roads.

The war ended, and he came home. The Poles took over the administration, and they were very much in need of technicians. And the Poles came, and in Sanok there was a construction bureau. A construction bureau which was involved in precisely these things. The construction bureau came and asked my father to come, since he was an expert in these things—

CN: Civil engineer.

SN: Yes. He was primarily responsible for materials. Let's say you need to build a bridge, and the bridge is so wide and so long—how much wood do you need? And he would figure it out.

So my father worked in the construction bureau. And there began to be pogroms in the surrounding towns. A pogrom in Cracow, a pogrom in Rzseszow. And one time my father came to work, and the chief, who was named Varim, said to my father, "There's going to be a pogrom in town." As there should be in a proper town. "The expensive things you should hide, and leave the rest to them."

And people began saying quite openly that there was about to be a pogrom in town. But there was no pogrom in Sanok. We had *zkhus oves*. What is *zkhus oves*?

CN: *The merit of . . .*

SN: *. . . the fathers.* As I told you last time, Sanok was a city full of out-of-towners. A Jew from Russia, from Gomel,[12] happened to find his way to Sanok. Why did a Jew from Gomel come to Sanok? In Gomel there had been a pogrom in 1903. There was one pogrom there in 1903. This Jew's name was Yudovitsh. And he didn't look like a Jew, but like a *katsap*. You know what a *katsap* is—a Russian, from deep Russia. He was a tall Jew, with shoulders from here to here, such broad shoulders! And with a mustache which reached to—you know the big Russian mustache.

When I saw him, I said "He must be a Gentile." And I saw him later, and noticed that sometimes he came to pray. "What's a *katsap* doing at the services?"

Yudovitsh began speaking, and in Yudovitsh's merit . . . Oh

12. City in Belorussia, also known as Homel.

yes, in 1903 he had killed a Gentile. He was a barber by profession, and he always carried an open razor in his pocket. So in 1903, when the pogrom came, a *pogromtshik* came up to him and stuck a knife into his arm. He sliced open the pogromtshik's neck. He was arrested, and he was tried, but somehow he got out of it. He argued self-defense. He sat in prison a few months, and that was it.

In 1905 there was a second pogrom in Gomel. 1905 was the year of the revolution in Russia, you know. A bigger pogrom in Gomel, and this time *he did better*. He killed two Gentiles. He was caught. He had cut the throats of two Gentiles, and in fact two pogromtshiks.

This time they decided, "We can't let him go free. Soon he'll kill the whole town, all of Russia. He's already killed a few Gentiles, there won't be a single Russian left!"

This time he was sentenced to heavy *katorge*—you know what *katorge* is?

JB: Hard labor.

SN: Hard labor.

JB: And exile?

SN: To Siberia. But you know, a Jew will always figure something out. He escaped, and came to Sanok, settled in Sanok.

So: The atmosphere of pogrom continued in Sanok, and the rabbi decided that we had to do something, we had to do something . . . The rabbi decided to declare a public fast, that people should fast for a day and say Psalms all day. The rabbi's understanding was that this was the best remedy against a pogrom.

But this Yudovitsh had a different opinion. There was a public meeting in the town synagogue, and Yudovitsh said, "Maybe that's good for the rabbi, but not for us. If only it were true that

Psalms could help, and a fast could help. And a fast isn't bad," he said, "it's a good thing. Let Jews eat a bit less." There was hunger in those years. "But," he said, "we must take other measures."

People asked him, you know, it was a mass meeting: "What other measures can we take?"

"I can't say that in public," he said. "If you want to know something about it, let's gather at a secret meeting. We'll discuss it further there."

It was announced that there would be a meeting of *ex-military personnel*, that is, people who had been in the army, and who knew how to hold a gun. "And where this will take place," he said, "I can't tell," because he was afraid the Poles would come and arrest the people as rebels, conspirators . . .

I wanted very much to go. I saw that my father was getting ready to go, and I said at home, "Let me come." But he wouldn't take me along.

When Yudovitsh came to the meeting, he said, "Leave it in my hands. I've had experience. I know what needs to be done in a pogrom. I know well what needs to be done in a pogrom."

First of all, he made a list of all the people who had served in the military. My father, and many, many more . . . there were almost a thousand Jews in Sanok who had served in the military. All of them young men. So he made a list of all these men.

Next—the Polish government had issued an order. Everyone who returned from the war with rifles, revolvers and so forth, hand grenades, must immediately surrender everything to the municipal military office. There was a heavy fine against anyone who didn't surrender their weapons. He said, "For God's sake, do not surrender a single rifle, don't surrender a single revolver. What should people do with them? Hide them, in a garden, in a cellar, don't keep it in the kitchen, but don't surrender it. Who knows when it could be useful?"

He understood. You see, in Russia there was *samo-okhrana*.

Have you heard that word, "*samo-okhrana*"? Self-defense, the Jewish self-defense. The young people—the Bund[13] and other youth organizations.

So—he said, "Don't surrender a single rifle, a single revolver. Bury it."

Meanwhile the atmosphere grew more tense. You understand that?

JB, CN: Yeah, yeah, yeah.

SN: The public market was on Friday, always Friday. The Gentiles were saying that on such-and-such Friday—I remember that it was a Friday in February—the pogrom would take place in Sanok.

And as I said, I remember that my father hid a few things that we had—valuables, not so much, we were poor people, whatever we had had that was valuable my mother sold, trying to see that we had bread, you know about that. I told you that she had sold my father's shtrayml, and other such things. Mostly furniture— the good cupboards—we didn't have anything to eat.

So one Friday there was a secret meeting with those ex-soldiers, and I cried, I wanted to go with my father. "Stop crying, it won't do you any good. We're going to talk about things you wouldn't even understand. We're going to talk about practical matters, how we're actually going to defend the city."

The "city" was a Jewish neighborhood in the center of the city. You know, around the market was the Jewish neighborhood. The periphery, the side streets were—Gentiles. We lived on the border, where the Jewish street ended and the Gentile street began. That's where we lived. But our street was entirely Jewish, except for one Gentile, a decent Gentile, Opinsky was

13. A non-Communist, non-Zionist socialist movement which promoted Jewish cultural autonomy in Eastern Europe.

his name. This Opinsky was a tailor. And there was one other Polish woman who lived there, but she was a loose woman. She wasn't . . . Anyway.

My father came home from the secret meeting. They had worked out a plan to defend the city. There were close to a thousand men who had served in the military. Nu, not all of them could—you know, they had come home sick, not entirely stable mentally, in short, there were several hundred left. And these several hundred were given arms—revolvers. They didn't want to use rifles, because rifles would have been a provocation. It would have frightened the Christian population to suddenly see Jews walking with rifles. "What's this?" So we won't use rifles for the time being, only revolvers. Groups were divided up—you know, Jews are Jews: a *minyan*.[14] Ten men—a minyan of Jews. And somewhere, I don't know where, Yudovitsh bought flat cans. And into each can he poured a quart of kerosene. Then they were sealed. Each one of the men had one of these cans of kerosene. Do you know by now what happened?

The Gentiles were accustomed to coming to the market very early. And they brought what they brought. Generally they brought potatoes, various vegetables, chickens, geese, eggs, butter, and the like. That's what they brought.

This is the plan that was worked out, focusing on the main streets, the ones that led to the market. The market was a sort of large square in the middle of the town, and several roads led into the market, various roads led into the market, and the Gentiles came there on Fridays, on the roads, and every Gentile came with a wagon.

And generally the Gentiles came, and what was on the wagon? Generally there was hay and straw to feed the horses. After all, the horses got hungry, so the horses were unharnessed.

14. The minimal quorom of ten adult Jewish males required for complete public worship.

They took out—what do you call the thing they put in the horse's mouth?

JB: *Bit.*

SN: The *bit*, the bridle, and then they ate. They stood and ate hay, oats and other such things. Nu—do you see the plan yet, or don't you see it yet? The plan was like this: The market would be surrounded. Ten men hid—this one would hide in this house, this one would hide in this house, and this one at the gate. But they were to be in contact with each other, and keep a lookout. And someone would be at the market, wandering around the market. As soon as anything began at the market, some sort of commotion—let's say someone began robbing the stores—they were immediately to open up the cans of kerosene, go up to the wagons, pour the cans out onto them, light matches, and make a *"boyrey meorey hoeysh."* That was their cryptic language. You know what a *"boyrey meorey hoeysh"* is? At *Havdalah*[15] the blessing is said, *"boyrey meorey hoeysh."*

JB: A fire.

SN: Yeah, yeah, yeah, *boyrey meorey hoeysh*. That means, "He who creates *eysh*, fire." And that was the plan. Not to start a fire in only one place, but in various places, in several streets.

Well, let's say, in normal times the Gentiles came, unharnessed their horses, gave the horses food, and they—the Gentiles themselves went—where does a Gentile go?

JB: Into the tavern.

15. The ceremony marking the close of the Sabbath, which includes the lighting of entwined candles.

SN: Into the tavern. And they got drunk there. That Friday—let's say that critical Friday—came . . . Yes, first of all one other thing. Meanwhile we wanted to know, wanted very much to know whether the Ukrainians would also participate in the pogrom. Only the Poles said there would be a pogrom. We hadn't heard anything from the Ukrainians. A delegation was sent out to the Ukrainian leadership. I remember that my father was one of those that went, because my father knew Ukrainian well. During the war years he had learned well, he had been with Ukrainian soldiers, so he had learned Ukrainian well. And they began asking the leadership: "Will you not participate in this pogrom?"

"God forbid," they said, "we won't do that. We assure you that if it's at all possible we will help you. But we certainly will not participate."

They returned with the good news, so we knew that from the Ukrainian side we had nothing to worry about, we only had to keep an eye on the Poles. Normally between two and three thousand peasants came on a market day. That Friday—that critical Friday—very early, there was an outpouring, twice as many as usual. We watched very carefully; not a single person came from the Ukrainian villages. We could tell easily, because the Poles living among us dressed differently from the Ukrainians. The Ukrainians wore their national dress—such as the shirt over the pants, not tucked inside the pants. And with long, long hair. Like, for example, you [indicates Boyarin]—and even longer.

That Friday when we looked—there were twice as many Poles. Poles only; there were no Ukrainians. Meanwhile the minyans were still standing in their assigned places. I don't even remember where my father was. I forget—I'm thinking now, where was he, what minyan was he in? No.

The Gentiles came this time with empty wagons. They didn't bring any butter, no eggs, no chickens, no geese—why? Because they were coming only to take! Just with empty sacks. Each wagon had about ten empty sacks. Was there that much merchandise to take from the stores . . . ?

It was quiet. It was quiet. The Jews opened their stores, and many of them were—we called them *budkelekh*, those are sort of small booths.

JB: *Stalls.*

SN: *Stalls*, yes, that's the word. The Jews had been instructed: "You pretend that nothing's happening. Open the stores and so forth." So they opened up. My mother was very nervous. She knew what was about to happen: The Poles would begin beating, and there were really several thousand, probably three thousand and maybe even five thousand peasants came. With women. Women came as well. And my mother kept sending me out to spy and find out what was happening in the market. I ran into the market. I didn't see my father—my father was somewhere and I didn't see him. Looked for my father, wanted to see him, wanted to say something—couldn't find him.

I was at the market—I was near the market, not in the market, but near the market. I started going home, it was about ten o'clock in the morning, and suddenly—a commotion in the market! Someone had struck with a piece of iron and broken open the door of a store, a Jewish store, and begun taking *shnit-skhoyre* out of the store—do you know what *shnit-skhoyre* is?

CN: *Textiles.*

SN: Yeah, yeah, *linens.* And I stood, and suddenly I took a look—there was smoke! I looked—all over the market, here was smoke, there was smoke. The hay and the straw, you know, when that was ignited, it went up in flames . . . Nu, horses are very much afraid of fire. They panic. Nu, when the horses saw that there was fire behind them, what did they do?

JB: They ran!

SN: The horses suddenly ran! They took off! And as soon as the wagons began to burn, each Gentile began to think of his horse! His wagon! His horse was going to be burned? That's his fortune! So he ran after it.

The Gentiles ran after the horses, the horses ran out of the market through the streets, and the Gentiles ran after them, shouting, trying to catch . . . And the wagons were burning already, you know, they'd had a quart of kerosene poured onto them, these were wooden wagons filled with hay and straw. When the horses ran, one wagon bumped into another, and one wagon ignited the other. I tell you, it turned into—God should protect us! Horses were burned, wagons were burned, and there was no pogrom. On the contrary—the Jews gained somewhat out of it, because they found parts of wagons, various pieces. There was no pogrom.

Later there was a sort of pogrom. They wanted to satisfy the formalities. And the Polish Government carried out an investigation. How did it happen that suddenly wagons began burning? "We don't know a thing." The Poles went around asking. "Nobody knows a thing." The Jews gave this explanation to the magistrate: One wagon happened to start burning. A drunken peasant wanted to smoke his pipe—and he ignited a wagon. And you know how it is with straw and hay, from one wagon another one caught fire, and another one, and it turned into a panic. The horses panicked, and they ran, and the wagons bumped into each other . . .

But no one was accused, no one was accused, and the matter passed.

But in the shtetl there did take place, a good time later . . . Have you heard of General Haller?[16]

JB: Yes.

SN: Yes, you've heard of General Haller. His army came—they were called *"Hallertshikes."* Incidentally, there were American Poles among them. There were Poles from America, Poles from France and Poles from England, who came to help.

JB: Right-wing nationalists.

SN: Yeah, yeah. There were . . . I spoke to one who told me that he came from Buffalo. A *Hallertshik* who came from Buffalo.

Anyway, the Hallertshikes came to town later. A regiment. They didn't do anything, except this: they went around with scissors in their pockets, and whenever they saw a Jew they went up and cut off half of his beard, half of his beard, no more. And a whole townful of Jews went around in Sanok with their faces wrapped up. They were embarrassed, half a beard. And really— that's all the Hallertshikes did. They didn't rob, they didn't take anything, they didn't touch anyone—they didn't touch any women. That's the only thing they did, when they went around in the street.

But we lived to take revenge against them as well. You know, Jews in Sanok weren't passive Jews. As I told you once, Sanok is an old cultural center. An old Polish cultural center. The first Polish writer whom we know about was from Sanok. Gregorius Sanocensis. He was writing in the times when people wrote in Latin. He wrote his works in Latin.

Gregorius Sanocensis had a statue in Sanok, built in the gar-

16. Leader of an army of expatriate Poles who fought during the Polish-Soviet war.

den, the municipal park. There was a large municipal garden, a marvelous garden! Ach, that was a marvelous garden! The garden was named after Adam Mickiewicz, the Polish national poet. From all over Poland, from every city and village, earth was brought to the garden. An artificial mountain was built, and on the top was the statue of Gregorius Sanocensis. You understand what that means?

JB: Gregory from Sanok.

SN: From Sanok, yes. He had a beard. It was still in the Middle Ages then, in the Middle Ages he had a beard. The statue was made of bronze. So a bunch of Jews went and chopped off his beard with an axe. Chopped off his beard! And that same day the Poles began shouting: "Who chopped off the beard?"

And there was an investigation. The Gentiles, the Poles, claimed that it was clear that Jews had done it. The Jews retorted, "We did it? It was the Hallertshikes who did it. They saw a Jew with a beard in the street, and they cut! Such a nervy Jew standing there with a beautiful beard." Oh—the inscription was in Latin. "*Gregorius Sanocensis scriba*"—you know, in the old style, everything in Latin. Nu, what Hallertshik knew Latin? He thought it was a Jew. He saw such a beautiful beard, such a long beard as his, and he chopped that one off too!

The Poles understood that this was a Jewish joke, but what could they do? They couldn't prove it, and that's how it was left.

The Boycott

SN: But the tension remained. It was actually both economic and political. Trade in the city was entirely in the hands of Jews. Virtually anything for sale in the city was in the Jews' hands. And the Poles attempted to shift trade into Polish hands. There came—an organization was created—*Rozwoj*—have you ever heard the name *Rozwoj*?

JB, CN: No.

SN: That was the work of a Pole from America, damn him! Roman Dmowski came and said, "The only way to fight the Jews is with our pocketbooks, with our pocketbooks." And he came with a slogan: "*Swòj do swojego.*"

You know what that means? "Each one to his own." That means, "Poles, don't buy from"—whom?

JB: From Jews.

CN: A boycott.

SN: A boycott. *Swòj do swojego*, with that slogan. And the Polish Government supported this explicitly and publicly. They provided credit. And there was created a network of . . .

JB: Cooperatives.

SN: *Koło rolnicze*, it was called. *Koło* means a circle, *rolnicze* of peasants. A circle of peasants was created. And they opened businesses in the city. For example, in Sanok they opened a big business. The government gave them credit, and the intention was that things would be sold cheaper there, things would be sold cheaper there . . .

And they employed people there, Poles without any business experience whatsoever. You understand what that means? Jews saw wagons of merchandise being brought there, and they wrung their hands: "Woe is me, woe is me, what will the Jews earn their living from?" But the truth was that the managers of these stores didn't begin to know how to run a business! So they sold

out their inventory, and they didn't replenish the stock . . .
They didn't know, for example, that a certain product must be
ordered, and records must be kept, a certain amount of a certain
product was sold, more has to be brought . . . They didn't know
that. They sold and sold, and they sold out.

Later, when, let's say, a peasant came into the cooperative
and wanted to buy something, the manager was ashamed to say
he didn't have anything. Ultimately the Jews began selling more
to the cooperatives than they did to the Gentiles! The cooperative manager came secretly to my Uncle Itshe, who had a store,
and said, "Give me such and such amount of flour, and such and
such amount of sugar." And he stole over to the cooperative
with it, and sold it cheaper than he paid Uncle Itshe for it!
There they don't exploit, there aren't Jews there who take
profits—this is not for profit. And it was always that way.

So in the end, they all went bankrupt. In a month, or maybe
two months, an economic committee came, took a look—there
wasn't any money! "What's this, what's going on!" He'd taken
the money to the Jew, he had to pay the Jew for his merchandise.

The economic boycott was a failure, the "swój do swojego"
didn't work. They understood, finally they realized that trade
isn't such a simple thing. It's not as easy as "I'll give you, let's
say, a quart of kerosene, and you'll pay me such and such
amount." It has to be planned, you have to know what kind of
merchandise to have. What we call in America *marketing*, these
people didn't understand at all. Absolutely didn't understand.
And the cooperatives went bankrupt. Lost a great deal of
money, and they went back—to whom? They bought and traded
with the Jews. They came to the conclusion that after all the
Jew gave honest merchandise for a low price.

True, the leaders of the *cooperatives* wrote a protest to Warsaw,
and they argued very naively: "The Jews sell good merchandise
cheaply, and we cannot manage to compete with them."

The return came from Warsaw: "Perhaps you might learn from the Jews, and you too could sell good merchandise cheaply. What then—do you want to sell bad merchandise for high prices? Who will buy it from you?"

Time to Move On

SN: So the economic boycott was a complete failure. But meanwhile the year 1920 began. And the Bolshevik armies began approaching Sanok. And there began a political, a political . . . so to speak . . . Jews sympathize with whom?

CN: With the Bolsheviks.

SN: With the Bolsheviks, yes. You know, I remember that people went around with satiric pictures which showed—I still remember, because I had a very good memory—there was a bear, and on the bear is sitting—you know who the bear is?

JB: The bear is the Russian.

SN: The Russians, and on the bear is sitting a Jew with a beard and *peyes*,[17] with his fringes[18] flying. . . . And I remember the Polish, the rhyme which went around: "*Na niedźwiedźiu*—on the bear—*siedzi Mojsze*—sits Moyshe. / A *Ty świecie*—and you, world—*patrz i dziwiaj sie*[19]—look and be amazed." And so forth . . . I don't remember any more. These kinds of cartoons were spread around the town, and suddenly, you know, the name

17. Sidelocks.
18. The *tsitsith* or fringed corners of ritual garments worn by Orthodox Jewish males.
19. The last words are an archaic Polish usage, possibly reflecting the local dialect in Sanok at the time, rather than the language of the posters.

"Trotsky" made its appearance. Despite the fact that the Poles in town didn't know anything about Trotsky, suddenly people noticed: "Ah, Leiba Trotsky." You know, that's what Trotsky's name was, he was a Jew. "Leiba Trotsky."

And political anti-Semitism began. My father decided, "We can't stay any longer." I had an uncle in America, who had been here a long time already. He was a great-uncle, an uncle of my mother's. He had been here—what can I tell you, he used to boast, "*Ikh hob gevut far McKinley.*" He had voted for McKinley. When was McKinley, nobody remembers?

CN: My grandfather remembered when he was killed.

JB: 1911?

SN: No, no, no. The beginning . . . 1901 or something. So my uncle had already been here for a long time. My father wrote to this uncle, "It's impossible to remain here. Anti-Semitism is growing from day to day." Now there's something new, political anti-Semitism. The Jews are identified with whom?

JB: With the Bolshevik.

SN: With the Bolshevik, and people were terribly afraid that there would be . . . An affidavit came . . . What?

CN: I think it was in the mid-nineteen . . . 1890 he died. He was . . .

SN: He was killed.

CN: A *veteran* of the *Civil War*, McKinley.[20]

20. President William McKinley was assassinated at the Pan-American Exposition in Buffalo, New York, on September 6, 1901.

SN: In short, my father received a paper, and he left. That was in 1920. I was already almost fifteen years old. I was born in July 1905, and in the beginning of 19 . . . or the end of 1919, my father left for America. When he left, we were like everyone, we didn't have any money. And we stayed at home in poverty, great, great poverty.

They didn't want to let my father out of Poland. Poland didn't want to give him a passport, because they considered him a technician. They decided he . . . What?

JB: Like today in the Soviet Union?[21]

SN: Just like that, just like that, exactly, the precise analogy, right on target. He was put into the category of technician, and they won't let him out. They don't let that sort out of Poland. My father said, "What do you have against me? You hate Jews, you want to drive them out, and me you want to keep here," because he had expertise in building highways.

In short, my father stole away. First of all he went to Czechoslovakia, to Bratislava, and there in Bratislava he got stuck. The Polish consul didn't want to give him Polish papers. He had an idea. In the war my father had worked with Czechs, so he had learned Czech. And I've told you that he knew Ukrainian. In Bratislava there was a Ukrainian consul, and at that time the great pogroms in the Ukraine were going on. You've heard of the Petlyura pogroms?[22]

21. It was common for Jews to be forbidden to emigrate from the Soviet Union, on the pretext that the government had invested heavily in specialized training for them.

22. Simon Petlyura was a leader of the Ukrainian nationalist forces fighting against the Red Army during the Russian Civil War. During the course of the Civil War, numerous atrocities were committed against Jews, primarily by the anti-Communists. Petlyura was eventually assassinated by a Jewish immigrant in Paris.

JB: Yes.

SN: And the Ukrainian consul gave Ukrainian Jews visas—passports and visas. So my father . . .

JB: He was a White?

SN: Yes, the Free Ukrainians. My father shaved his beard. He left himself a mustache, and put on a cap. He put on a sort of worker's shirt, like the workers wear there, and he went to the Ukrainian consulate. He said that he was a Ukrainian refugee, that he had run away from the pogroms, and they started questioning him. They asked, "Where do you come from?"

In the war years my father had been in the Ukraine. He was a soldier in a city called Radziwilow. It's near the border. So since he knew the city, he said, "I'm from Radziwilow."

It turned out that, unfortunately, the consul was *also* from Radziwilow! But my father knew the city; he had been there for a long time. So he was asked, "What street did you live on?" And he mentioned a certain street.

"Yes, there really is such a street. Did you know there a certain family named Lerner, the family Lerner?"

My father said "Yes, I knew the family Lerner." He said, "The old Lerner was a rabbi." In short, my father came to America with a Ukrainian passport, as a Ukrainian.

But my father came here, and took a look around, and the situation there did not improve, it grew worse. So my father writes to me, I was just about fifteen years old, he says, "I think, my son, that you should come to America. I don't have any money to bring the family." People earned very little in those days. "Until I earn enough money—"

COMMENTARY

Three themes stand out in this chapter. The first, continuing earlier concerns, is the internal development of Jewish society. The second is the volatile situation of an ethnic minority located at the fault line between territories claimed by two competing national movements—in this case, Ukrainians and Poles. The third, expressed in the pogrom narrative, has to do with two kinds of violence—symbolic and physical—and with strategies of resistance to that violence.

Curiously enough, while Noble stresses the flowering of Jewish organizational life immediately after the end of the war and lists a number of the new groups, he offers us no narratives about their activities or about the competition among them. For his part, young Noble was still willing to sit and study in a yeshiva, as long as it was acknowledged that he personally was a *daytsh*, someone with skeptical and modern inclinations.

Although scholars commonly speak of "Jews and the surrounding population" as if everyone among whom Jews lived were identical to each other, in Eastern Europe it was more common for Jews to be part of a contentiously multiethnic society. The Chmielnicki massacres of 1648–49 were committed against Jews by Ukrainians as part of a revolt against the Polish nobility, which had colonized the Ukraine and set up Jews as business agents. When Poland became independent, the Jews of Sanok were once again caught in between.

But Noble's family was as prepared for this confrontation as any members of a relatively weak ethnic minority could be, since they lived on an ethnic border within Sanok, "where the Jewish street ended and the Gentile street began." His memories of Gentile neighbors are particularized rather than stereotypical: one was a prostitute, the other an honest tailor. The sense of common humanity that Noble managed to acquire in his childhood may help explain his willingness to compare his grandfather's piety to that of a Catholic bishop without the term of separation—*lehavdil*—that he had earlier used to distinguish between human beings and horses.

In any case the Jews' ability to make distinctions among their Gentile neighbors—to tell whether there were Ukrainians among the pogromists, for example, by noting what they were wearing—was helpful in a crisis. In fact, along with the mutual hostilities and prejudices shared by Jews and various Gentile groups there were lines of communication that are also in evidence here, such as the advance warning that a pogrom was about to take place.

The hindsight of sixty years perhaps helped Shlomo Noble to discuss the attempted pogrom—"as there should be in a proper town"—with a bit of detached irony. This aside, however, also indicates Noble's awareness that the wave of pogroms was not simply an irrational manifestation of eternal anti-Semitism, but rather part of the chauvinist nationalism attendant on the achievement of Polish independence. Retrospectively, it is a gentle way of reminding the listener and the reader that the Nazi genocide had its own prehistory in the decades immediately before World War II. On the other hand, the planned violence had a social meaning beyond its victimization of Jews and beyond any loot that might be acquired. Through their active abjection of Jews, the Poles of the Sanok region were to align themselves unambiguously with the Poles of the entire nation-state, against the local Ukrainians and Jews. This also helps to explain why the Ukrainians failed to participate.

The Jewish strategy of creating panic among the peasants' horses is a breathtakingly creative example of what the scholar James Scott calls "weapons of the weak."[23] Noble employs various metaphors of value in describing the character of the newcomer Yudovitsh and the preparations for the Jewish self-defense. Neither Noble in his narration, nor Yudovitsh in the narrated address to the assembled Jewish men, directly derides the traditional methods of prayer and fasting, but diplomatically suggests that they need to be supplemented. Some Jews in Sanok might, in fact, have attributed the averted pogrom to the merit of the fathers. Noble clearly attributes it to the merit of the stranger Yudovitsh, who is so far from

23. James Scott, *Weapons of the Weak: Everyday Forms of Peasant Resistance in Southeast Asia* (New Haven: Yale University Press, 1985).

representing the traditional image of a meritorious ancestor that he is frequently mistaken for a Gentile, by both Jews and non-Jews. In summarizing Yudovitsh's career before coming to Sanok, Noble says that during the second pogrom in Gomel, "*he did better*. He killed two Gentiles." The Americanism here indicates a very modern, secular idea of achievement. When contrasted with the rabbi's plan for penitence and supplication, the figure of Yudovitsh and his success encapsulates the "modern Jew," consistent with the range of Zionist and Jewish socialist organizations described elsewhere in the chapter. Yet the language used to describe the organization of the self-defense—the minyan as the unit, the *boyrey meorey hoeysh* as the action—suggests a continuity between traditional forms of Jewish solidarity and the new thinking the pogrom threat called for.

The Jewish response to the later "pogrom" that actually did take place—the rampage in which General Haller's soldiers cut off Jewish men's beards—similarly lies somewhere between the sensibilities of the rabbi and of Yudovitsh. Cutting off beards is a physical act, but it is certainly symbolic violence as well, an attack not so much on the lives of Jews as on that which visibly marks them as Jews. To chop off the beard on the statue of Gregory Sanocensis in return was to twist the joke back on the anti-Semites: it was a parodic act of "symbolic symbolic violence." To claim that the soldiers must have thought the statue was a Jew was, of course, a kind of "Polish joke," a suggestion that they were too obsessed with stereotypes to see the difference between a human being and stone. But to remind the Poles that their own national hero had worn a beard was also to remind them that Jews, despite whatever marked them as different now, were human too.

Like the defeat of the pogrom, the failure of the cooperatives represents an ancient theme of wit triumphing over numbers. What is handed down to us are images: the young child learning the difference between the dots on the page and the melody sung by his teacher; the huge number of peasants converging on the marketplace, which Noble conveys by simple redundancy; the vandalized statue in the town park. The spoils of wit's triumph, however, are not territory but the wisdom of communication.

4

To and Fro Across the Sea of Memory

SN: Close the door, and we will talk.

General Examination

SN: What I wanted to tell first of all is—children, remember, as I've already described, I studied with Reb Meirl for a short time, and then left right for America. But this was told to me by my brother who studied in the yeshiva many years later. He told me this. I told you that a Jew by the name of Itsik Hertsog had given a building to the yeshiva. That's how the yeshiva began—he gave a building.

This man was a very simple Jew. But he had provided the building. There was a board of trustees. He was one of the trustees. They had to give him some honor. He was a very simple Jew, Itsik Hertsog. Very simple. I don't even know how such boorishness could survive in Sanok. But this Jew possessed it. He didn't know a thing. He knew how to pray, of course, perhaps he was able to read the Bible a bit . . .

95

The other trustees were all extraordinary scholars, the finest scholars in town. There was Weingarten—his name was, yes, Weingarten; there was another trustee named Gottlieb; scholarly Jews, fine scholars.

So he [Hertsog] complained to Reb Meirl: "All the other trustees are addressed with the honorific title 'Reb': Reb Yidl Weingarten, Reb Mordkhe Gottlieb. Me they call 'Itsik.' How come they don't call me 'Reb'?"

So [Reb Meirl] proclaimed: From now on everyone must say 'Reb.' All the trustees alike shall be called 'Reb.'

But one time he came and complained to Reb Meirl: "The yeshiva boys don't give me any respect. They treat the others with respect." But not him—they treated him like a common Jew.

So he asked: "What do you mean, they don't give you any respect?"

He answered: "They don't say 'Good morning, Reb Itsik' to me. They say 'Good morning.' "

He said: "What can we do?"

He said: "I have a . . . I know what to do." There was a sort of board. He wrote on the board himself: "From today on *makhriz umodiye* . . . " Do you know what that means? That's how every announcement in the yeshiva begins. *Makhriz*—it is called out; *umodiye*—and it is announced, that from now on all the students must say, "Good morning, Reb Itsik." That's what he himself wrote: "Good morning, Reb Itsik."

Well, the boys saw that, and they said, "We'll figure out what to do." They hid an entire day, and they didn't see him. They saw him, but they avoided him. But in the evening, when he came from *maariv*,[1] all the boys lined up every fifteen steps—

CN: Good *morning*, Reb Itsik.

1. The regular evening service.

SN: Good morning, Reb Itsik! And then another one—you know, every fifteen steps stood another boy: "Good morning, Reb Itsik!"

He became very, very angry. "They're mocking me." He announced that there would be a general examination for all the students, as a punishment.

JB: The *rosh yeshiva*,[2] that is.

SN: No, no, no. He did this, the trustee.

So it was like this—but remember, I'm telling you all this only as my brother told it to me. Not one of the students took it seriously. You know—"Reb Itsik, Reb Itsik" didn't know a thing. "General examination." People passed by and saw the announcement, and they were incredulous: "General examination"!

My brother is really quite a joker. He has a remarkable sense of humor. He said that he wanted to say a *pilpul*.[3] You know what a *pilpul* is?

CN, JB: Yes.

SN: He wanted to say a pilpul. There is a Mishnah in Sabbath, in the Gemore of Sabbath. A situation is described there, and the exact wording is *hoyo roykhev al gabe beheyme*.[4] Someone *hoyo roykhev*—was riding; *al gabe*, on the back; *beheyme*, of an animal, usually a kind of cattle. There the word *gabe* means "the back of an animal," but as you know, the same word spelled differently means "a trustee."

So my brother said, "I want to say a pilpul on *hoyo roykhev al gabe beheyme*. *Gabe beheyme*—this presents a problem already.

2. The director of the yeshiva.
3. Here, a virtuoso display of Talmudic textual analysis.
4. In fact this phrase appears in Mishnah Baba Metsia 2.

There's a contradiction in terms here. If he's a *gabe*—then how can he be a *beheyme?*[5] And if he's a *beheyme*—then who made him a *gabe?*"

He [Itsik] didn't understand it. Reb Meir bent into his Gemore, at his lectern, and laughed quietly, so that he wouldn't see.

My brother said, "There's a difficult Rambam[6] on this topic," he cited a Rambam, and he brought in citations from *Sefer Pralnik*[7]—you know what *Sefer Pralnik* is? And the crowd rolled with laughter.

And he turned to my brother and pinched his cheek, and said, "Well said, but you just shouldn't be a wise guy." Well, that was one incident from the General Examination.

Prison

SN: The second [thing] I wanted to tell you was about what?

CN: Yudovitsh.

SN: Oh yes, Yudovitsh.

In Sanok there was a marvelous garden where people went walking. That's what it was called: *shpatsir-gortn*. Once it had belonged to a Jew—Reb Abba Shulkaner, the town rabbi. He was a tall Jew, this Reb Abba Shulkaner. He had married a rich woman, and the garden belonged to him. People told him that in his garden young people, boys and girls, went walking on the Sabbath, Friday night, after supper . . .

---

5. "*Beheyme*" in Yiddish came to mean more specifically a cow, but is also used as an epithet for a stupid person. The words meaning "the back of the beast" thus come to be translated "the trustee is a fool."

6. The Hebrew name for Maimonides; here "a Rambam" means a passage in Maimonides' Jewish law code.

7. A book of parody sermons for Purim, published by M.A. Kugel in 1899 in Lemberg.

"Really?" he said. "I'll give the garden away, I don't want it."
And he gave it to the city. It became a municipal garden. And
they made it very beautiful. It was like this: The path was
twisted, it kind of snaked around, up and up and up to the peak.
And in between flowers grew.

I was once arrested for walking through the flowers. It was
forbidden, but I was in a big hurry and I walked through the
flowers. I was taken to the police. I was a small boy! I sat there
waiting for my hearing. Meanwhile the policeman came in and
gave a report about Yudovitsh. There was some sort of commotion, a commotion in town, some Gentiles got drunk and were
fighting with Jews, and Yudovitsh had cut several Gentiles with
his straight razor. He opened it up and—he was very agile—in a
wink he'd cut a long gash in someone's face.

So a policeman came in and gave a report about Yudovitsh.
He said that it had taken place in the street, Jews and Gentiles
were fighting . . . The lieutenant said to him—I don't know
what he was, I didn't know then—either a lieutenant or a sergeant—and he said to the policeman, "And where were you,
son of a bitch, where were you? Why did you let it happen?"

The policeman said, "Sir, I looked at the fellow, and I
thought he looked like *nashe*, I thought he was one of ours. Not
a bit of a beard, no sidelocks . . . "

Yudovitsh was already a revolutionary, let's say one of the Russian revolutionaries. Dressed like a Gentile, you know, in a cap
. . . So he said, "Sir, I thought he was *nashe*, I thought he was
one of ours. But suddenly," he said, "I looked—oh no! He's
cutting Gentiles' faces, not Jews'! So I ran up and arrested him."
He said that he had cut maybe ten men's faces.

But what I want to tell you is how naively the policeman
answered, "I thought he was one of ours." If he was one of
"ours"—probably he was hitting Jews. Probably he was cutting
Jews. Then he saw that—"Oh," he said, "suddenly I looked and
I saw he was cutting the faces of Gentiles! So I took him away."

That's all I wanted to tell you about him. We won't return to Europe anymore.

Goodbye to Beards and Socialism

SN: I'm already on the way to America. I went to Warsaw to take care of my visa, to get my passport in order. I've told you that I was in Hashomer Hatsair. The whole time I was in Warsaw my headquarters, so to speak, was Hashomer Hatsair. There I became friendly with a girl in Hashomer Hatsair, Lyuba Shabrinsky. She was from a wealthy family. Her father had a large leather business on one of the finest streets in Warsaw, the main street actually, Marszalkowska. Lyuba was some two or three years older than me. Once she invited me to their house for Friday night dinner. I was delighted to accept the invitation. When I arrived, I saw that it was a very fine house. It was still a very strictly traditional home. I had a very good time. Meanwhile there was a boy there, a small boy also—maybe I've told you about that small boy, Kid Luzer, no?

CN: No.[8]

SN: There was a small boy there; Lyuba told me that he was from the Ukraine. Actually he wasn't much younger than me, maybe a year, but he was quite immature, and didn't have, you know—because of the war years, the pogroms, he couldn't read, absolutely nothing, was completely illiterate.

The problem was—yes, his mother—he had a father here in America, but his mother died just about that time. Killed in a pogrom in the Ukraine. "The boy wants to go join his father in America, but they won't let him, they say he's not capable of

---

8. Noble never did tell us about Kid Luzer.

taking care of himself." Would I want to take him along with me? I was how old then?

JB: Fifteen.

SN: Fifteen years. But on the other hand, I could read, I could write, I could speak, I was no slouch. I wasn't bashful, and so forth. So I said, "Yes, certainly." But somehow it didn't work out. They didn't want to entrust him to me, they said he was too young. But I got to know this boy. I remember I went with him several times, and spoke on his behalf, but they said that a fifteen-year-old wasn't dependable. Nothing came of it. I forgot about the boy entirely. Years later—it was in 1924, my father was living in a town, Nashua, New Hampshire. Do you know Nashua, New Hampshire?

CN: I've been there.

SN: One summer I came to visit my father in Nashua. And I was bored, bored, bored—terrible. A small town, there's no, you know . . . And my father said to me, "There's a Jew, a very interesting Jew, a rich Jew, a wealthy Jew. His name is Shaber. Go over to him. He has a very fine library. By the way," my father said, "he's a very interesting person. He's a Jew who began his career as a Bundist, a social revolutionary Bundist, and he even went to prison on account of his Bundism, and now he's in America. He forgot about Bundism a long time ago, he forgot about prison too, and he's a very wealthy man."

I went to this Jew Shaber and I said: "Mr. Shaber, my father said that you have a library, and you'll let me look into your library . . . "

So he said, "One minute." Meanwhile, I looked at the wall—there's a picture of a Jew with a long beard down to here. And a yarmulke, a big yarmulke. A fine-looking Jew, an elderly Jew.

And I looked at the picture, and he said, "Why are you look-ing at that picture?"

I said, "Somehow I know that picture."

"Where did you see that picture? Eh—" he said, "you're imag-ining it. You know that all Jews with beards look—"

"No, no, not all Jews with beards look alike. I remember that Jew very, very . . . " And I began—I have a good memory—I began to think, where have I seen that picture? Where have I seen that picture?

I hadn't seen it; understand—you see already that Shaber and Shabrinsky are the same—

JB: Yeah, yeah.

SN: But I didn't see it. I thought that Shabrinsky was Shabrin-sky, and Shaber was Shaber. Suddenly I said, "Oh! You know I was in Warsaw at the home of a Jew named Shabrinsky. And he had the exact same—"

"Oh!" shouted the man, and he began shouting, "Kaye, Kaye, come in, this young man knows my brother in Warsaw." The one who was Shabrinsky in Warsaw became Shaber here in America.

Eh—it's a long story, I won't tell you the long story. I got to know him very well. We became very good friends. He wanted to give me money to travel to Cincinnati and study at the Re-form rabbinical seminary. I said no, that I had already studied enough. I didn't accept his proposal.

But one time I asked him—we became very good friends—I said to him . . . yes: At that time there was a factory in Nashua which made—you remember, once upon a time there was net-ting, mosquito nets. And there was a strike then. And Shaber gave money to break the strike. He helped the owners. Once I asked him: "Mr. Shaber, I can't understand it. How is it that in Russia you were a Bundist, a social revolutionary, and went into prison in order to help other people. And here you've suddenly become so . . . How can it be?"

He said, "No. I've—" we spoke Yiddish, we only spoke Yiddish—"I've worked myself up to a higher unity."

I said, "What is this higher unity?" You know, I thought it was something philosophical, some sort of abstract unity.

He took out a dollar and he said, "You see? Here it says, '*E pluribus unum.*' From many has become one. And that has become my higher unity. That's what I believe in, and I've been successful at it. I'm quite successful." He said it quite simply.

I'll just tell you—he wanted to give me a check for ten thousand dollars to travel to Cincinnati and become a Reform rabbi. But I said, "No, no. I've had enough."

COMMENTARY

Noble's narrative was not strictly chronological. The first and last of the three vignettes in this chapter are related to Noble's departure from Europe and voyage to America—an episode which he chose not to relate to us in comprehensive detail. The second is an amplification of the story about the averted pogrom.

Although Noble was not in Sanok during the yeshiva students' encounter with "Reb" Itsik, the story is told as vividly as if he had actually been present. Doubtless his familiarity with the setting, and his brother's vivid and enthusiastic retelling, made it possible for him to pass it on to us, third parties, half a century later. In addition to its inherent humor, the story anticipates run-ins that Noble will have with the administration of the yeshiva he attends in New York. The boys' strategy is a classic ruse to point out the abuse of power. They take an arbitrary rule and follow it in an entirely inappropriate way, with opposite results from those intended by those who promulgated it. The story also reveals an important bit of cultural history: at least in the yeshiva world, not every adult Jewish male was considered entitled to the honorific "Reb."

The story of "Reb" Itsik recalls a similar anecdote contained in the memoirs of Yisroel Kopelov,[9] who was born in Lithuania a decade or so before Noble. Kopelov tells of an ignorant village Jew who came to the synagogue in town only on the High Holidays, when he had to suffer the nickname "Zalmen the Goy." After Zalmen complained to the rabbi, the latter decreed that no one was to call Zalmen a Goy any longer. The congregation complied, and began calling him "Zalmen the Jew" instead!

I have no doubt that Polish peasants and members of the urban working classes were capable of such linguistic subversion as well. In Noble's account, however, such resources lie with the Jews, whereas Gentiles are constantly handicapped by language. Thus in returning to Yudovitsh, Noble does not merely describe, but actu-

9. *Amol iz geven* (New York: Max Meisel, 1911).

ally performs the monolingualism of the policeman: "I thought he looked like *nashe* [ours in Polish], I thought he was one of ours." A Jew, telling the story, is master of the Pole's idiom as well as his own; the Pole, the storyteller claims, is so limited to his own world that he can't distinguish a Jew from a stereotype. His cultural blindness is represented by his confinement to his own idiom. Only the Polish word "*nashe*" can create this meaning here, ironically betraying at the same time the blatant discrimination practiced by such "civil servants."

On the surface, Noble's meeting with Shabrinsky/Shaber might seem simply to hang on a remarkable coincidence: in far-off New Hampshire, meeting the brother of a man Noble happened to meet in Warsaw. In fact, the burden of this sketch is to stress that Shabrinsky and Shaber really are *not* the same. The brother in Warsaw is still religious; the one now in America, when living in Europe, had been a Bundist, a Jewish socialist. Religious practice aspires to a unity or harmony with the divine; socialism aspires to universal unity among human beings. Neither ethos resembles the possessive individualism epitomized by Shaber's claim that the *E pluribus unum* slogan on the dollar bill represents a "higher unity." For the Shabrinsky who has become Shaber, every dollar is interchangeable—and this is more important than the rights or welfare of any obstreperous workers.

Noble's stories, on the other hand, retain an insistent particularity, signaled here by their refusal to come together into a neatly unified chapter. Noble does not explicitly condemn the sea change in Shaber's worldview, but his later stories of his years in America amply demonstrate that Noble never altogether abandoned the values of Judaism and of an ethical socialism.

5

In Beaver Falls

SN: I came to America. It was, I remember it was 1920, a week or two before Thanksgiving, because I remember I already ate turkey in America, I was taught the word "turkey." So that's how we can determine it.

Arrived at a small town in Pennsylvania, Beaver Falls. Today everybody knows about Beaver Falls, where do you know about Beaver Falls from? Joe Namath is from Beaver Falls. Once upon a time when I used to say Beaver Falls to someone, they'd laugh at me. They thought I'd made it up. I arrived in Beaver Falls, a town with seventy or seventy-five Jewish families. But they had a synagogue, and they had a Talmud Torah. My father actually taught in the Talmud Torah, he was one of the teachers. I arrived, it was . . .

JB: That was his livelihood.

SN: No, then, just then. Later he changed. You know, at first people didn't know the language, and had to . . .

JB: I'm interested generally in the way your father got to the smaller towns.

SN: Yes, yes. My father arrived in America, and he didn't know a word of English. He didn't have a trade. He had to wait. There was a paper in New York at that time called the *Tageblatt*. The *Tageblatt* carried Help Wanted announcements. He read that there was a town called Beaver Falls, seventy families and so forth, and they were looking for a second teacher in the Talmud Torah. And my father figured—"Meanwhile I need a livelihood, I can't sit idle." So he went to Beaver Falls.

American Logic

SN: The other teacher was a Jew who'd already been in America for many years, Khayem Sidler. Khayemke Sidler. And now I'm going to tell you about Khayemke Sidler. It was already almost evening when I first arrived. And I remember we ate, and my father said, "I'm going to introduce you to Khayemke Sidler."

Khayemke Sidler came into our house. And Khayemke Sidler said to me, "You know what? I'll teach you English. I'll teach you English."

Certainly. It was very good with Khayemke Sidler. However, he spoke English with the *sabesdike losn*.[1] He was, you know, a Litvak, and he spoke English with the *sabesdike losn*. I didn't know. I thought that everybody, everybody, speaks that way. I didn't know a word of English. I remember he took me for a

---

1. The Yiddish dialect in large regions of the Lithuanian Jewish culture area does not make a consistent phonemic distinction between s and sh. The two sounds are therefore confused, collapsed and/or contrasted, but in reverse positions to those they are voiced in by other dialects. Thus, for example, *sabes* instead of *shabes*, "Sabbath," and *losn* instead of *loshn*, "language." This paradigmatic example provides *sabesdike losn* as the popular name for this dialectal trait.

walk in the evening, and as we were walking, he said, "Where shall we begin? Oh: I'll teach you to count. To count. That's very important," he said. "You know, because if you don't know counting, you could be swindled, you go into a store, they'll rob you. Repeat after me," he said, "*Van.*"

And I repeated, "*Van.*"

"*Tshoo.*"

And I said, "*tshoo.*"

"Three, four, five, six, seven, eight, nine, *tshen.*" He didn't say "ten," but "*tshen*" was what he said, "*tshen.*" Tsh, tsh, a sort of soft . . . "*Tshen.*"

And I repeated, "*Tshen.*" Nu—it didn't take long until I learned it, *van, tshoo,* up to *tshen.* He didn't teach me any more.

"Nu," he said, "what else do you need to know? Yes," he said, "how do you call things—in the house? There's a *kitsen* and a *paller.*" He meant parlor, but he said *paller.* "And a bedroom."

And I repeated, a "*kitsen,* and a *paller,* and a *bedroom.*"

"Yes, very good, very good," and he continued teaching me. Now this Khayemke was somewhat of a philologist as well. He loved to show off his wisdom. He said to me, "Nu, do you know what a *kitsen* is now?"

I said, "Yes, what we call a *kikh* in Europe."

He said, "Just see how logical English is. A *kitsen* and a *tsiken* have the same letters. However, *tsiken* has the opposite accent. *Kitse-e-en,* and on the other hand *tsikn.* What's the connection?" he said. "Because in a *kitsen* you cook a *tsiken.*"

And I repeated—you know, that was his pedagogy. You had to repeat everything. "In a *kitsen* you cook a *tsikn,* and a *tsikn* is called a *tsikn* because it's cooked in a *kitsen.*"

Nu—and so forth, and then he said to me, "This is very important; you have to know what the various meals are called. In the morning people eat *breakfast.* Because people eat so quickly, they break, break, break the *crackers*—" at that time people ate crackers for breakfast—"and so they call it *breakfast:* Break fast!"

"The English language is very, very logical," he said. "Everything with reason. Lunch is called *dinner*." He said, "They eat it so fast" that there's thunder, thunder, thunder.[2] "So you see already how it's all done with reason, carefully thought out. What's eaten in the evening is *supper*, supper. Why *supper*?" He said, "People come home from work, from the shop so exhausted that they *sapen*." You know what *sapen* means—[pants]. "People pant. Everything," he said, "is logical here in America. Everything is done with reason."

I learned everything, and I enjoyed this discipline. He explained things very clearly.

Thursday evening he came again and he gave me a lesson in— as he said it—*rifmetic. Van* and *van*—

JB: *Tshoo.*

SN: *Tshoo.* And so forth. Up to twenty he counted up. Very good. It was really . . . Afterward he taught me practical things. He said, "For example, you go into a *store*, and you have to know what to say."

I said, "What's a *store*?"

He said, "A *store* is a"—I've forgotten everything already— "a *krom*."

I said, "A *krom* is a *store*. Very good."

"But not every *store* is a *store*. There's a *drogshtor*," he said. He said, "*shtor*." "There's a *drogshtor*, and there's a *furnitsur shtor*," and he explained to me everything that there was, there's a *furnitsur shtor*, and there's a *shtor* . . . "But one thing," he said, "is an exception. A *groshery*. You don't say *shtor*, you say *groshery*."

And indeed I learned a good deal. Meanwhile Friday came,

2. *Duner* in standard and Lithuanian Yiddish; *diner* in Galician Yiddish and other non-Lithuanian dialects.

Friday night was the Sabbath, so I didn't have a lesson. Friday night my father said to me, "Come, we'll go visit a family I know." They were young people by the name of Markson. He actually had a *furnitsur shtor*. And the Marksons had both been born in America, young people, about thirty years old. They had just been married. Both born in America. But they still spoke Yiddish quite well, it's interesting. Everybody—even the American born—spoke Yiddish in Beaver Falls. Even the young people. Even if their Yiddish wasn't so good, still they spoke Yiddish with their parents. The parents knew very little English.

So this Markson, who was a very friendly person, asked me, "What are you doing? Are you studying something?"

I said, "Yes. Khayemke Sidler is teaching me English."

They burst out laughing. I said, "What is it?"

"He speaks English? He doesn't even begin to know a word of English!"

Khayemke did a little peddling on the side. In Pennsylvania at that time there were very, very strict Sunday Blue Laws.[3] Khayemke didn't know a thing about it. He went out on Sunday and did some peddling. You know, from town to town. So a policeman stopped him and gave him a summons, of course: "Violation of the Sunday Blue Laws." Have you heard of Sunday Blue Laws?

JB: Yeah, yeah, yeah.

SN: They only had them in Pennsylvania. In New York there were no . .

CN, JB: In New Jersey they have them.

CN: A very pious state, New Jersey.

3. Laws regulating the closing of businesses on Sunday.

SN: I live in New Jersey now. I don't know if it's a pious state, but very, very polite. It rained in New Jersey this morning, and a drop fell down on me and said, "Excuse me."

In any case—he didn't understand the policeman. He came to Markson. "God help me, I don't know what he's talking about. He gave me some sort of summons, I don't know what for." So they explained to the policeman that Khayemke didn't understand English.

Incidentally, Khayemke told me that he had come to America in 1890. It was thirty years later already, and he still didn't know any English.

CN: My great-grandfather—one of my great-grandfathers came when he was about forty years old, and he was on the Lower East Side. And after forty years in America, he was eighty years old, the postman asked him, "What's your name?" and he didn't know how to answer. He needed a translation . . .

SN: It was that way with Khayemke too. Khayemke came from Lithuania, of course, and the first day he became a Hebrew teacher. Khayemke came to Beaver Falls from . . . Oh yes, Malden, Massachusetts. And in Malden, Massachusetts, there were already a large number of Jews at that time. And he only spoke Yiddish with the children. And in the Talmud Torah only Yiddish was spoken.

My father said to me once, "Go into his class. He teaches Bible." I'll never forget it.

I remember he was teaching the Bible portion that begins with the words *Lekh lekho*.[4] The standard translation was, "God said to Abraham, get thee out of thy country," and that's how he taught it, with the old European intonation. He had been told to modernize his teaching a little bit. "Okay, okay, I under-

4. Genesis 12:1.

stand," he said. *"Lekh lekho*—get outta here; *meyartskho*—from your country; *umoladkho el haorets asher areko. Agadlo shimekho"* which means, "And I will make great your name," he rendered, "And I will *advertayzn* your name." That was the American way of doing it.

So when I told them that Khayemke was Americanizing me, they just laughed.

Solomon's School Days

SN: In short—the resulting decision was that I was to go to school. On Monday my father took me to public school. The public school in Beaver Falls was the most backward in all America. Beaver Falls had, you know, foreigners, only foreigners, Poles and others . . . It was a manufacturing town. Virtually the entire city belonged to the Mellons, the Mellons of Pittsburgh, and the others, Carnegie . . . Well, the people there were an immigrant population, workers, so they figured that whatever they gave them was enough for the children.

Terribly backward. You'll hear in a minute how backward. I seem to remember that they were still reading from the *McGuffey Readers*. And the reason I remember is that there was a story which I later saw in the *McGuffey Readers*, a story with a dog named Spark, and other such wonderful things: "Spark, run. See Spark run," and so forth.

CN: I also had a stupid reader when I was in public school.

SN: Yes?

CN: A dog Spot. Run, Spot.

JB: Run, Dick, Run. I had *Dick and Jane*.

CN: For me it was very, very boring in public school.

SN: Yes? And by the way I was older than all the other children. The other children were six years old, in the first grade. And a teacher who was an idiot, truly an idiot. Miss Caughy—first of all, Caughy: C-a-u-g-h-y. And I couldn't say Miss *Kay*, I had to say Miss *Kagy*. And she teased me to make me say Miss *Kagy*, not Miss *Kay*. In short—I came in, the first day, and they were studying by looking at a picture. There was a picture, with a girl and a boy and a dog. We spent the entire day—these children had never even had a book in front of their eyes—they spent an entire day on one lesson. And I was bored, bored, bored, and when I came home, I said, "Father, at the rate I'm going," I said, "the way I'm learning now, the Messiah will certainly come long before I learn English. And certainly Messiah will come, so why do I have to learn English? We'll all have to go to Erets Yisroel, and there we'll have to speak the Holy Tongue!"

My father said, "What can we do?"

So that's how it was the first day, the second day, the third day . . . One time I said to her—I had already picked up a few words: "*Miss Caughy, I take book home.*" I'll take the book to my house.

She said, "Yes." Usually the children didn't take the books, they left the books there. I took the book home. It was the weekend, a Friday, and all day Sunday I sat and learned the entire book. How well did I learn it? . . . but whenever I didn't understand a word, I asked, and one of the children in the house told me.

So Monday came, and I told her I'd studied the whole book.

"Really?" she said. She didn't believe me. She was going to question me. She asked me what Spark was doing.

I said, "Spark barks."

"Oh—you know already." Now, she said, she was going to teach me arithmetic. Probably I didn't know arithmetic. She said to me, "How much is one and one?" I didn't know what *one and one* was, because I was used to saying—what?

JB, CN: *Von and von.*

SN: No, *van and van.* So I said, "I don't know."
  She said, "Aha, you see? You don't know any arithmetic." And she began drawing the numbers . . .
  "Oh," I said, "*van* and *van*—that's *tshoo.*"
  Yes. One thing I forgot to tell you. I wanted people to call me Shloyme and nothing else. That's what I'm called today, Shloyme. Absolutely not. She said, "It can't be done, it's impossible." She told me that there was a law—one had to have an English name. She called me "Solomon," and I hated the name "Solomon" with a passion, I hated it.
  So: "You see, Solomon, you don't know arithmetic. First of all, it's not *van*, but *one*. One and one is not *tshoo*, but two." You know, I'd gotten so used to that *tshoo*, that I didn't get myself out of it. It took quite some time before I got away from those Lithuanianisms of his, that *sabesdike losn* of his. But it went away eventually.
  When I saw what "arithmetic" was, I said, "I know multiplication and I know division . . ." I forgot to tell you. When I was in Hashomer Hatsair—still in Sanok—there was a young fellow around my age. His name was Kimel. Kimel wanted very much to learn Hebrew.
  Kimel went to gymnasium.[5] "Tell you what," he said. "You teach me Hebrew. And as many hours as you give me of Hebrew, I'll give you in general, secular studies. I'll lend you my books." He taught me, and I studied with Kimel like this for an entire year. I don't know how much Hebrew I taught him, but I learned enough so that I went to take an examination, and I

5. A European secondary school.

received permission to enter . . . I received credit for three years in gymnasium. Three years in gymnasium was the equivalent of fifth, sixth, and seventh grade.

So I said to Miss Caughy, "I know . . . this"—I didn't know the word multiplication—"and I know this"—division. And I said to her, "I even know a little . . . I've studied *alegerla.*"

JB: *Alegerla.*

SN: *Alegerla,* yes, algebra. In short, she didn't know what to do. But finally she decided that I was to be in the fourth grade. She sent me into the fourth grade. And there it was a pleasure: in that grade, in the fourth grade, it was entirely the opposite. The teacher there was Miss Brown. And this Miss Brown . . . I must admit, children, I almost fell in love with this Miss Brown. It made one feel good to be near her . . .

JB: I was also in love with my teacher in that grade.

SN: So you understand. This Miss Brown said, "You know what, Solomon"—she too called me Solomon, and she suggested that I read a collection of simple biographies. *American Great Men,* it was called. Have you seen this series, more or less? About George Washington, you know—he only told the truth; and about Benjamin Franklin and others. And I absolutely devoured this. I didn't understand everything, of course, but whatever I didn't understand I asked about. And they explained it to me, and it was fine. And this was really how I learned English.

I forgot to tell you about a very comic moment. In the first grade there was—it was called *physical culture, physical exercise* or something like that. The children—it was like this, the children were paired up. Then they held hands and stretched this way and that way. For me there was no partner. After all, these were six-year-old children. She [Miss Caughy] said, "You know what,

Solomon? I'll exercise with you." I thought, an old Gentile woman, what's . . . you know, we were standing there like . . . I'll show you . . . [moves.] The children pull each other's arms like this. And one time she really pulled, and she let go of my arms, and she fell down.

She got very angry. And I remember that she gave me a bad mark in conduct. And she complained—and my father came, she complained to my father that I . . . He said, "What does bad *konekt* mean?"

In short, I left her, thank God, from there, and the fourth grade was a pleasure. I didn't take part in the class, but I sat the whole time, since Miss Brown understood that I would profit more from reading on my own, rather than following along in the fourth grade reader. And in this way I would really learn something, gain some conception of American history. So I read that, and I remembered it.

In short, I had it good in fourth grade. I still remember one incident. Valentine's Day was approaching, and a girl came up. A very pretty girl, about ten years old, fourth grade, you know, ten years, and she gave me a card that said, "Be my *Valentin*."[6] I said, "What does that mean? What is this? What am I supposed to do?" And I came running, and asked the children: "A girl gave me a card, and on it was written, as you see: *Be my Valentin*."

They said, "Oh, it's nothing. It's a game, kids, *Valentine's Day*." I became very afraid.

I enjoyed myself very much. And as I said, I almost fell in love with the teacher, Miss Brown. One time I heard people saying something about a *party*, we had to give Miss Brown a *present*. I didn't know. You know what it's like for children: partly I did understand, partly I didn't understand what that meant, that we had to give the teacher a *present*. I began asking,

6. In telling the story here, Noble places the emphasis on the second syllable.

and it turned out she was going to get married, and she was going away to Lancaster. That's what she told me later. She took me aside, and she told me that she was going. "However," she told me, "I'm going to promote you to the sixth grade."

On Account of a Calf

SN: I had been in sixth grade for a few weeks, when an incident took place which brings us back to the town.

Oh yes, I remember what it was, yeah. The richest Jew in town was named Solomon. This Solomon, like almost all the Jews there, had a store. But he had worked himself up and bought himself a mine. He had bought a burned-out pit. The company didn't use it anymore, but there was still a good deal of coal in it. In that region it was the bituminous coal, the soft coal. He bought the mine, and things worked out, he was successful.

Solomon had a Bar Mitzvah—a son of his became Bar Mitzvah. He had invited—he had a large family. Invited cousins and second cousins. You know, in those times family loyalty was still . . . It's very interesting, I want you to know this. Today family loyalty has become quite lax. I have cousins whom I haven't seen for years and years. I have cousins, and I really don't know whether they're still living. But then it wasn't this way. Then there was still a strong loyalty. When a holiday came, let's say, when Passover came, people went to their grandmother, a whole family, and there would be thirty-odd children, and it was lively, people slept on the floor.

So, Solomon invited his uncles and aunts and brothers-in-law. And you know, he was somewhat stingy. He thought to himself that if he went to buy the meat from the butcher, the butcher would figure the retail price. In that time there were still many farmers around Beaver Falls. Indeed, in Beaver Falls itself

there were farmers. And he bought a calf. Bought a calf, probably paid four or five dollars for the calf, and he figured he would
get a hundred pounds of meat from the calf. But he had to get it
slaughtered, of course.

In Beaver Falls there was a Jewish slaughterer named Traub.
He was a slaughterer, but he also had a butcher shop. And he
sold meat there, but not only kosher meat—he sold non-kosher
meat as well, in the same butcher shop. My father, who was very
strictly religious, found that very objectionable. Because according to the law, as you probably know, if you sell kosher meat
and nonkosher meat together, you can make a mistake. You
know, put a piece of meat here instead of there, change the
knives around . . .

JB: Mix up the blood . . .

SN: Mix up the blood, in short, everything, you know, by
mistake.

CN: There was a similar incident in my neighborhood, on the
Upper West Side. A butcher had a nonkosher fish store in one
half, and a kosher butcher shop in the other half of the store.
There were protests, and he had to take away his "kosher" sign.
Yeah, and . . .

SN: In short, that was how Traub had it set up. And in our
case, my father was the only one who ever reacted. And there
were several men there who were quite religious, and he spoke
to them once: "I don't know," he said. "In Europe," he said, "it
wouldn't be permitted. In Europe would they permit a butcher
to sell kosher meat and nonkosher meat in the same store?"

Now, this is how my father and I happened to witness Traub
slaughtering Solomon's calf: In Beaver Falls the custom was to
hold a minyan only on Shabbes and on holidays. And Friday

night. Friday night, Shabbes morning, and holidays there was a minyan. During the week, regular weekdays, there was no min- yan. But if a Jew had *yortsayt*,[7] people would go—and the Jew who had yortsayt would go and knock on the door: "Yortsayt!" So people knew already, today there's, today—we have to make a minyan today.

And incidentally—this is I must tell you, it's quite lovely. There was a Jew there—his name was Hilke, Hillel probably, and he was called Hilke, Hilke Cohen. Hilke Cohen had a terri- ble passion, may it not infect us! You know, Gentiles have pas- sions, and Jews have passions, but there's a difference. A Gentile has a passion—he yearns to take a drink. A Jew has a passion— he yearns to lead the congregation in prayer. He loved to lead the congregation in prayer. He had a beautiful voice, this Hilke Cohen. So several times a year he would come, [knocks on desk] "Yortsayt for my mother! Yortsayt for my father!" A week later, "Yortsayt for my mother" again.

We got him out of the habit. One time a cynical Jew said, "Actually, it's possible to have several fathers. But mothers— how could that be?"

He saw that people had realized he was imagining yortsayt so that he could have an opportunity . . . To him it was the greatest pleasure to stand up there [sings]: "*Moyshe viamru anu . . .*"[8] And in fact he had a very fine voice.

Once there was a yortsayt of this type, and my father called me to come along, simply because in a small town it's hard to get ten people.

And precisely that day when we went to pray Solomon came

7. The anniversary of the death of an immediate family member, when an adult male Jew is required to recite the Kaddish memorial prayer in the presence of a minyan.

8. Either Noble's citation is inexact, or my transcription here is faulty. It is plausible, and poetically fitting, to assume that he is referring to the passage just before the daily Amidah, which the ArtScroll Siddur renders, "Moses and the children of Israel exclaimed a song to You with great joy . . ."

along. He brought the calf in a small truck. And right by the synagogue there was a small room where animals could be slaughtered. But nothing big, you couldn't slaughter big animals there. There wasn't enough room. But a small calf you could. And mostly *tsikens* were slaughtered there, for the *kitsen*.

So—Traub the slaughterer also came to the minyan. And after the service the slaughterer went outside, and I waited with my father. And Solomon said to my father, "Mr. Noble, I'm going in the same direction, I'll take you home." He said, "Why should you wait for the streetcar?" Incidentally, the streetcar was called a *jitney*. He said, "I'll take you. Why should you wait for the jitney?"

[*Editor's note*: The end of this story is not on tape. Noble describes how the calf's throat was cut once, after which the calf was still alive and attempted to escape. Since the laws of kashrut require that the animal be killed with a single, uninterrupted motion of the knife against the jugular vein, there was no way this could have been a kosher slaughter. Yet when the calf's throat was then cut once again, the carcass was nevertheless declared kosher. See Noble's explanation of *shehiye*, "interruption," below.]

This incident resulted in a religious trial. Rabbi Kazin from Pittsburgh came to Beaver Falls. Incidentally, he was a very modest man. You probably haven't heard of him; he passed away afterward. But you probably know his nephew. Alfred was his nephew. A very capable person. The uncle was also very capable, a fine scholar, and a modest man. When he came to Beaver Falls, he quoted the statement from the Ethics of the Fathers: "*al tihi don yikhid*"[9]—a single individual shouldn't stand in judgment. He said that he wanted to have two more Jews—scholarly

9. Mishnah Avot 4:9.

Jews, of course—and he asked the president of the synagogue whether there were some Jews there who were capable scholars.

The president said, "Yes. There is a Jew, his name is Noble. And another Jew named Solomon [?]." And he asked my father to come and serve on the religious court. My father agreed, of course. That's how I know what happened: I heard my father talking about what had happened at this trial.

So everyone came to the trial, and the first question Rabbi Kazin asked the slaughterer—this *Reverend* Traub, as they called him—was, "How long has it been since you looked into *Tvues shor?*"[10]

Tvues shor is a handbook for slaughterers. We have one here. We never had *Tvues shor* before, I had *Tvues shor* at home. The second edition, incidentally, of *Tvues shor*, and I presented it here. Look at *Tvues shor*, because there are diagrams there showing how the animals look internally; they are wonderful. Imagine—they're from the seventeenth century. But really precise. I once asked a veterinarian whether it was anatomically accurate. "Absolutely," he said. "Very well depicted."

So he asked him, "How long has it been since you looked at *Tvues shor?*"

He thought a little bit, and then he said, "A few years."

Rabbi Kazin said, "According to the law, according to the *Shulchan Aruch*,[11] a slaughterer is supposed to go through the laws of kosher slaughter every three months. If not, you know, one forgets." He said, "And you're telling me a few years already . . ."

So. The slaughterer didn't say anything. Didn't answer at all. Oh yes—he did respond. He said, "I'm very busy. I have to take

10. This book, by Reb Alexander Sender Shor, was first printed in Poland in 1633.

11. The code of Jewish law written by Rabbi Joseph Karo in the sixteenth century and, with commentary and adaptation by Reb Moshe Isserles, accepted as authoritative by Ashkenazic Jews.

care of the slaughter, and I have a kosher butcher shop and a nonkosher butcher shop."

"Really?" he said. "Now we're getting to the point," he said. "You have a kosher butcher shop and a nonkosher butcher shop in the same store?"

"Yes," he said, "but on separate tables. There's a kosher table over here, and a nonkosher table over there."

Good. Two negative points already. The third point, he said to him, asked him, I'll explain it to you: Do you know what *shiye* is? I told you last time, *shehiye*, spelled *shin-hey-yud-hey*.

JB: Tell us again.

SN: Tell you again—*shehiye*: interrupt. Once you've begun slaughtering, you have to go back and forth. And not stop in the middle.

So he said, "Do you know what *shehiye* is?"

And Traub answered, "No, I don't know what *shehiye* is."

He saw by then that there was nothing else to say. He had asked him three simple questions, and he hadn't answered a single one of them. He thought it over a little bit, Rabbi Kazin— and he was a very fine man, a very good man, and he said to him, "Reverend Traub, I'm afraid that you will have to give up slaughter. And you must not slaughter until you come again either before me or before another rabbinical court."

And that's how it was. My father told me about it when he came home. Incidentally, my father wrote the report. My father was able to write very well and very fast.

It was announced that from now on the slaughterer must not—oh yes, in addition, he said, "You will have to give up one of your butcher shops. Either you will sell"—

SN, JB: Kosher meat or nonkosher meat.

SN: One of the two.

And—nu, what does God do? In Pittsburgh there was a large community, there were seventy or eighty thousand Jews in Pittsburgh in those years. And there was another Orthodox rabbi in town. His name was Sivitz, Rabbi Sivitz. And, as is usually the case with two Orthodox rabbis, they didn't get along with each other. They constantly argued, had various disputes . . . This Traub picked himself up and went to Rabbi Sivitz. And he came back to Pittsburgh with a smile on his face, and he pulled out— he couldn't read, he actually didn't know what was written there, but he understood that it was all taken care of. "Oh, that Rabbi Sivitz," he told everybody, "he's a scholar, he's a judge, he's a *mumkhe*, an expert," and so on and so forth. And he came to show it to my father. And my father fell silent.

I've told you that my father stopped eating meat at that time . . . But he said the reason was that he'd had a dream in which he'd taken a vow not to eat any meat for a certain period of time. And that was why he wasn't eating meat. He didn't want to say that it was because . . .

Okay. That's one thing. Now you know what happened with Rabbi Kazin. Meanwhile there was a tumult in town. He showed people [the letter] from Rabbi Sivitz. These people—practically nobody could read. Perhaps there were a couple who could read. And for those who could read it was a surprise: "He says he's a scholar?" He praised him [Traub] to the skies.

In short—there was a feud. People argued while they were praying, people argued at home. Relatives and friends stopped talking to each other. Fathers-in-law stopped talking to their sons-in-law. And one Lithuanian Jew, a Jew from Vilna, went home on account of this affair. Really, I'm telling you, he really went home. He lived with his daughter, and his daughter was only interested in one opinion. She said, "If Sivitz said he's a good slaughterer, why should I doubt it?"

And one Jew shouted, "And to hell with the chief Rabbi

Kazin. To hell with the chief Rabbi Kazin," he said, "what do we need him for?"

And darkness fell, darkness! It went so far that one time there was a fight in the synagogue, Saturday afternoon during the afternoon prayers, and the slaughterer went up to a Jew, an old Jew, the first Jew to have settled in Beaver Falls. Lazvus was his name. He gave Lazvus a shot, and he broke his glasses. And such a tumult broke out, as you can understand. The police came into the synagogue, and all account of this. Nu—there was a government trial, they came before the judge there, the judge didn't begin to understand what it was about: What are they talking about here? What is this—he did slaughter properly, he didn't slaughter properly?

JB: What's the question—the animal was dead!

SN: Yeah, nu, yeah. Something else I have to tell you. It was said in town that he had brought along a large sum of money and left it on Sivitz's table. That's what people said; I don't know.

And it went on like this, it became such a dispute in town. I tell you, everybody suffered from it. The Talmud Torah suffered from it, my father, people didn't want to send their children to the Talmud Torah anymore. Yeah.

JB: Did he stop being a slaughterer?

SN: No!

CN: But what did Rabbi Kazin's followers do for meat?

SN: It wasn't far from Pittsburgh, only thirty miles. And on the other side was Newcastle, Pennsylvania, and there was a kosher butcher there as well. And people went to Newcastle. But my father didn't want to eat either one's meat.

Meanwhile, as I told you, the whole thing came about because a Jew named Solomon made a Bar Mitzvah, and he slaughtered the calf for the Bar Mitzvah. He wanted to hang onto a couple of dollars, and he slaughtered the calf. And with that one calf the trouble began.

We received an invitation, my father and I, to come to the Bar Mitzvah feast. My father said, "I can't refuse." He was a decent man, this Solomon, a simple Jew, really, he didn't understand a thing, a rich Jew. My father said, "We can't refuse. I'll go, but I won't eat anything. I'll only eat a piece of fish, I suppose that I can eat, and whatever else there is on the side I'll eat, but I won't eat anything made of meat." And to me he said, "You do what you want. If you want to eat, you can say that you're one of those who follows Rabbi Sivitz."

We came to the feast. I'm only telling you this on account of how I came to the yeshiva. There was a young man at the Bar Mitzvah, a young man from Chicago, a few years older than me. I got to know this young man, and I liked him very, very much. We talked and talked. I asked the young man, "What do you do?"

He said, "Oh, I study in the Yeshiva Itzkhak Elkhonon."[12]

I said, "Oh, that's in New York."

He said, "Yes."

I asked him to tell me something of the yeshiva. "What should I tell you?" he said. "It's what Volozhin was like once upon a time. It's like Slobodke[13] used to be. Precious," he said, "an institution that's a pleasure."

And he spoke about the yeshiva with such enthusiasm that I went home and said to my father, "Father, I've decided to go to New York." This was three or four weeks before Passover, in the week of Purim.

12. The formal name is Rabbi Isaac Elhanan Theological Seminary. Founded in 1897, it was the forerunner of Yeshiva University, and is now the rabbinical school of that institution.
13. Volozhin and Slobodke were two of the greatest Lithuanian yeshivas.

JB: In what year?

SN: 1921. I began in 1921. This was in February or March 1921.

JB: You were in Beaver Falls for one year.

SN: Yes, yes. So my father said, "By all means." He said, "I'm very satisfied," he said. "Meanwhile," he continued, "you know—I've decided that I don't want to be here."

I asked him what bothered him about the place.

My father said, "In a community where there is no peace, there is no blessing. Where there is no peace, there is no blessing. I am afraid," he said, "that the synagogue will fall apart." He said that all the people had withdrawn, sometimes there was barely a minyan.

You may ask, "What was Traub the slaughterer doing?" He didn't come to pray. He didn't come to pray. By the way people really ostracized him, I think, since he had slapped Lazvus. The president said to him, "You should be ashamed. A Jew who raises his hand against an old man is an evil man. An evil man." But he continued, he was a slaughterer and so forth.

Meanwhile we didn't have a cantor, there was no cantor, my father had to lead the prayers, it wasn't . . . My father said, "You know what, I've decided I'm going to leave too. I don't want to be here anymore."

I said, "Why not, Father?"

"A community where there is no peace—there is no blessing there." That's what my father said. Like it was a rule, a principle, that it was accepted, that people knew it. And a week before Passover, I remember, we went away. My father gave up his position, said that he was going away, and we traveled to New York.

COMMENTARY

Beaver Falls presents an instructive contrast to Sanok in the first decades of this century. Here again the themes of internal Jewish difference and of ethnic boundaries between Jews and non-Jews are prominent. Yet in Sanok, the internal Jewish differences represented an efflorescence of Jewish life; here, the conflict over kashrut led to communal dissolution. In Sanok, the ethnic boundaries were mortally dangerous; in Beaver Falls, they were only culturally painful.

Consistent with Noble's lifelong professional and personal interest in cultural history, he marks his coming to America by the word "turkey," which he learned shortly after arrival. Quite likely the taste of a new food further reinforced that memory. The identification with Thanksgiving and with the year 1920 represents a conjuncture of the repetitive annual cycle of festivals and the passing linear time of history books and biographies. Although Noble does not emphasize this, the proximity of his arrival to Thanksgiving also places his immigration within the mythic space of the Pilgrims' voyage to America.

Noble rarely indulges in standard cultural stereotypes, which makes it all the more startling when he does. One such case, apparently, is his flat statement that Gentiles have a passion for drinking, Jews a passion for praying. This distinction represents an old and well-established stereotype among Jews, exemplified by the well-known and much-lamented ditty, *Shikur iz a goy* . . . ("A Gentile is a drunkard . . ."). Possibly Noble shared this stereotype, or else he was playing with it ironically, to emphasize Jewish foibles; probably both elements are present.

Other passions begin to enter the story for the first time in this chapter, albeit quite innocently. The celebration of Valentine's Day must have made Noble nervous in more ways than he relates here. Certainly it was a strange custom; something was being asked of him, and he didn't know what it was. Noble presents himself as being utterly baffled. Yet the motif of hearts may well have clued even this greenhorn in to the fact that it had something to do with love, with which he had little experience even in a traditional Jewish context, let alone secular, Gentile America. On top of that, here was a sixteen-year-old boy in a classroom full of ten-year-olds. When one of them asked him to be her Valentine, how could he possibly have reacted appropriately, especially knowing as little English as he did? Besides, by then his heart belonged to Miss Brown.

Noble makes clear that part of his trouble in public school stemmed from his faulty education in English within the small Jewish community. The extended discussion of Khayemke Sidler's instruction is presented as an example of the structured misunderstandings that often occur at cultural borders. Sidler's explanation of the relation between "*kitsen*" and "*tsikn*" (the latter a stock example of Lithuanian Jewish pronuciation in America) is particularly rich. They are neither English nor Yiddish, but examples of a nonce-language somewhere in between. Doubtless Noble featured this example of his would-be teacher's style because it represents a double parody of Lithuanian Yiddish and of the famed Lithuanian Jewish "analytic reasoning." The example of folk etymology is likewise characteristic of Noble's interest in the way traditional Jews understood the larger world in which they lived.

Khayemke also serves as a mouthpiece for images of America as fast and brash. Breakfast is so named because you have to break your food quickly; supper, because you're so tired from working that you pant. The vernacular translation for God's "Get thee out" is "Get out of here!" and "I will make great your name" becomes "I will advertise you."

Noble states that it took him some time to rid himself of such Lithuanian Yiddish influences in his pronunciation of English. As an adult, however, his English was altogether standard. And in any case, during our recording sessions he was speaking in Yiddish. Yet twice during the session in which he spoke about Khayemke he introduced *khayemkeisms* into his narrative. First, in describing the person who explained to Noble that Khayemke was not the best teacher he could find, Noble says "and this Jew actually had a *furnitsur shtor*." Much later—long after leaving the subject of Khayemke—in describing a butcher shop, Noble says "mostly *tsikens* were slaughtered there, for the *kitsen*."

Certainly these latter two cases represent deliberate stylistic choices, and not lapses on Noble's part. To say that he used them for humorous effect is obvious and inadequate. Why is this amusing? In these two moments, Noble the storyteller impersonates the character Khayemke—or, to put it differently, the character Khayemke is allowed to speak through the storyteller. Noble knows himself and the worlds he has lived through well enough that he need not suppress Khayemke. Here, fleetingly, but more forcefully than in the earlier extended description of the character, "the spoken word is uttered as a reminder, like memory enacting some primordial contact"[14]—we meet Khayemke and listen to him.

The story of the slaughterer illustrates common tensions in small-town American Jewish life at the turn of the century. How effective was rabbinic authority once the community had lost its authoritative sanction? In Sanok, the pretensions of the rich Jew Itsik Hertsog had been successfully mocked by the yeshiva students, with the collusion of the head of the yeshiva. In Beaver Falls, the ones who seem to prevail are the "rich, decent, simple Jew" and the butcher who colluded with him in passing off a badly slaughtered calf as kosher. Partly because of such tensions—which caused dedicated religious Jews such as Noble's father to return to the larger cities—but much more because of external demographic forces, small-town American Orthodox Jewish life is largely a thing of the past. Whether the failure to find peace results from interethnic conflict or more intimate quarrels, the maxim "Where there is no peace, there is no blessing" is an apt ending for this chapter. Whatever the saying's immediate source may be, it brings to mind Rabbi Simeon ben Halafta's statement recorded at the end of the Mishnaic tractate *Uktsin* 3:12:

> The Holy One, blessed be He, found no vessel that could contain blessing for Israel save that of peace, as it is said: 'The Lord will give strength unto his people; the Lord will bless his people in peace.'

14. Paul Zumthor, "The Text and the Voice," in *New Literary History* 16 (1984), p. 74.

6

The Yeshiva in New York

Love at First

SN: And we arrived in New York. It was the first time I'd been in New York, just before Passover, and it made a terribly negative impression on me. *Vey, vey, vey.* You know—people threw everything out of their houses into the street, in the street. The sidewalks were filled with old beds, broken beds, mattresses . . . feathers flew from all sides . . .

JB: On account of Passover.

SN: On account of Passover, yes, yes.
   The intermediate days were the registration period in the yeshiva. At that time the Yeshiva Itskhak Elkhonon was conducted according to the European system. Two semesters. One semester precisely from Passover until Rosh Hashanah, and the second semester from after Sukkot until Passover. In the week of Passover there was vacation, and the entire month of Tishrei there was vacation.
   In short, I arrived in the yeshiva during the week of Passover.

I was given both a written examination and an oral examination. And apparently I was quite successful in the examination, because they began to—in the yeshiva there were two parts. There was a rabbinical, that is, the yeshiva proper, and there was a *bes medresh lemoyrim*, for teachers, the Teachers' Institute, TI, as they called it. So there was an argument; the registrar from Teachers' Institute wanted me to go there. Why? "Because he knows Hebrew very well, and we need that kind of student. He already knows it."

I myself said, "No, I want to go to the yeshiva." The difference was this: in the yeshiva they studied Gemore for six hours every day, from nine until twelve, and—no, not six: from nine until twelve, is three; from one until three-thirty. That is, five and a half hours. In *bes medresh* they only studied Gemore for two hours every day. And that was a big difference. In addition they taught pedagogy, they taught, you know, methodology, and that sort of thing.

I said I only wanted to go to the yeshiva. They accepted me at the yeshiva, and I began with a phenomenal enthusiasm for the yeshiva, with a phenomenal, phenomenal diligence. I wanted to learn. As much as they studied there, the first few weeks, as much as it was, it wasn't enough for me.

I lived with my uncle, my Uncle Moshe, and that was about a half hour one way—an hour's walk there and back.

JB: Was it already in Washington Heights?

SN: No, no, it was still in . . . When I arrived the yeshiva was on Montgomery Street. You know Montgomery Street?

JB: Yes, on the East Side.

SN: Then, when I had been there a few weeks, it moved to East Broadway. East Broadway and Cannon Street, in a big building.

And I had the *hasmode*—you know what *hasmode* is, *masmid geven*, studious, studious, eager, eager, eager to learn—for me an hour's walk there and back was Torah time wasted, I lost time . . . So I asked them to let me move into the yeshiva. The yeshiva didn't have a special dormitory.

However, students lived on the fifth floor. And in addition here and there were small rooms which couldn't be used for classrooms, small rooms a bit larger than this one. And they gave them to students to live in.

I came along and I told the administration of the yeshiva that I wanted to live in the yeshiva, I have a right to it: I'm from out of town. They said to me, "Unfortunately, there is nothing. There's no room. All the rooms are occupied. As soon as there's room—" they would give it to me.

Meanwhile I heard that one of the boys, a young man who came from Vancouver, had begun to show signs of neurosis. A young boy, fifteen or sixteen years old. He was homesick, he had never been away from home, and there he was. No doubt the lifestyles in New York and in Vancouver were probably quite different. There was no way he could get used to it. It was hoo, ha, running here and there. Vancouver is probably a small town. I've never been there.

JB: Like from Hotzenplotz[1] to Warsaw.

SN: Yeah, from Hotzenplotz into Warsaw.

He got drunk, began crying and began showing other symptoms. He couldn't eat, lost his appetite, lost weight. And the doctor—they had a doctor who used to come in, and he said, "You know what? Go home to Vancouver. I'm afraid . . . In two or three years you'll be a bit more mature."

1. Hotzenplotz, the name of an actual small town in Eastern Europe, is used in Yiddish the way "Podunk" is used in American English.

I received his room. But I had to—the room was on the second floor, near the library, right across from the library. Ah, did
I enjoy myself! The library was never locked at night, and I sat
for entire nights in the library, and studied. Nu—and I was very
happy. No matter how many hours we studied, I didn't have
enough. I would sit by myself later, and study all night long, and
just learned . . .

And I became acquainted with [Bernard] Revel.

JB: He was the rosh yeshiva, or . . .

SN: He was the president of the yeshiva. My rosh yeshiva was a
Jew by the name of Flaks. But this Flaks left soon. I only studied
one tractate with him—Ketubot.[2]

CN: The trustees at that time were German Jews or Russian
Jews?

SN: All Russian Jews. There was no sign of a German.

And—yes, Flaks left, and I went into the class of a man
named Levine. Levine was a bizarre man. Really a bizarre man.
A fantastic—ooh, ooh, ooh, a fantastic teacher, a rich Jew, and
somehow he was especially fond of me. I know why: my diligence, he saw me as a really devoted student.

And Revel liked me very much. Whenever he met me, he
asked me, "And are you satisfied?"

"Oh, Dr. Revel," I said, "satisfied. And how! And how am I
satisfied!" I said.

We'd talk a bit, until I said, "I don't want to talk too much,
it's time wasted from the Torah, it's wrong. When one can be
studying, one should be actually studying, not talking."

Nu—we had a synagogue in the yeshiva for the students. You

---

2. The *ketuba* is the Jewish wedding contract.

know, a sort of chapel. We prayed there. Those—only those who lived in the yeshiva. We had to get up an hour early in the morning in order to go to the minyan. There was a *gabe* who would wake us up, went around and knocked on doors: "Minyan time! Have to go to the minyan!" And the afternoon and evening prayers we prayed in a minyan, and on the Sabbath, Sabbath we prayed.

JB: And you ate.

SN: What?

JB: In the yeshiva.

SN: No, this is how it was. In the yeshiva we only received lunch. No breakfast—you had to get that for yourself. And in the evening it was the same thing.

If You Eat Pork . . .

SN: There was a board like this. On the board there were indicated [in Hebrew] the time of morning prayers, the time of afternoon prayers, Sabbath prayers, such and such a time. Entirely logical, of course. The bulletin board stood in front of the synagogue, in front of the entrance to the synagogue, in a prominent place, just when you came into the building. Once I came downstairs—I told you I lived on the second floor— and there wasn't any . . . "Oh, no!" I said. "What is this?"

Everything in English: "*Morning services,*" such and such time. "*Evening services,*" such and such time.

I thought, What happened here? What kind of revolution happened here? And what's more, you know—from left to right!

"*Sabbath prayers,*" such and such time.

The boy who was the gabe in the synagogue was from Philadelphia. I'll never forget his name. His name was Bar—Barnett. We called him "Barney" Barnett. So I ran to this Barnett and I was ready to simply tear off the notice. To tear the notice down. "What is this?" And I went up to him and I said to Barney—Barnett, "What's this—'Zman tefilas shakhris' is no good, so we have to write 'Morning services'?"

He said, "Don't get excited." He said, "Orders from the boss."

I said, "Boss? Revel ordered you. . . ? I can't understand it."

I want to tell you an episode with this—with this Barnett. I rode to America on a ship called the Gottland, White Star Line. On the ship there was a young man, much older than me, and I became very well acquainted with him. It turned out that he had been in all the Lithuanian yeshivas. He was one of the eternal students. Sat and learned and learned. Then he went from one yeshiva into a second, let's say from Volozhin to, let's say, Slobodke, from Slobodke to Mir, from Mir, you know, to some other yeshiva. And as I said, while on the ship I became very well acquainted with this young man, and—he didn't say anything about it, but I arrived in the yeshiva a few months later, and the young man was there in the yeshiva. He was there in the yeshiva. And when he saw me he embraced me, he was very, very friendly, and we became close. He told me, "I decided to become a rabbi here in America. This year I will be ordained." He had so much learning, more than most scholars. At that time he was the gabe, not Barnett, the one from Philadelphia. He was the gabe at that time.

Now, even on the ship, his behavior had been somewhat strange. But in the yeshiva he began to demonstrate somewhat odd behavior. One day he didn't say a word to anyone, he walked around . . . And we didn't know what it meant. We didn't understand that this was a kind of depression. He went around very melancholy, and even to me he didn't say anything. And later he would say bizarre things. Once on the Sabbath he

called up Barnett to recite the blessings before and after a portion of the Torah reading. And he said it like this: "*Yaamoyd—*"[3]

At that time there was a popular song, I remember it: [sings]
"Barney Google, with his googly, googly eyes." You've probably
heard this "Barney Google with his googly eyes"? It was a humorous thing, Barney Google had a horse named Sparkplug . . .

JB: Yes, I know it as a comic strip. Barney Google and Snuffy
Smith.

SN: Yes, yes, yes. Barney Google had a horse named Sparkplug,
[sings] "And when the horses ran that day, Sparkplug ran the
other way. Barney Google . . ." I heard it everywhere, you
know, it was a very popular song in the early twenties . . .

So this young man whom I knew from the ship stood up and
called out: "Yaamoyd, Barney ben Moreynu Reb Google."[4] Like
that. And Barney was very ashamed. And we didn't know how
to respond. Why are you laughing? [laughs] "Barney ben Moreynu Reb Google." And he started crying. This young man,
Barney Goo—was about my age, a year older, probably a year
older. And he started crying.

Meanwhile there was an uproar. A holy place, and it's being
turned into, what? Theater? And we students began banging on
our lecterns: "Down with the gabe! Down with the gabe!" And
we ran up, and we began to console Barney.

Barney was literally weeping, weeping with bitter tears. He
said, "Why do I deserve to be insulted? Everyone else is called
up properly. Then he comes to me, and they call me [laughs]
Barney ben Moreynu Reb Google." And he knew it was from
the song.

I remember there was a student by the name of Berman,

3. "Stand up," the beginning of the standard formula for calling a congregant to
the Torah.
4. "Barney, the son of our Master Mr. Google."

Shloyme Berman, who later died in Hebron in 1929, he was one of the . . . You know that in Hebron there was a yeshiva . . .

JB: Yes, yes.

SN: There were boys from our yeshiva who died then,[5] he and two brothers, and a—Hurwitz, four, the two brothers Horbater, is four. This Shloyme Berman was a fine young man, and he went up: "Sha, sha, sha, we shouldn't make any commotion, it's the Sabbath, don't make any commotion. Yaamoyd Ben-Tsion"—Barney's first name was Ben-Tsion—"Ben-Tsion ben Reb Mordkhe." That was proper form, and Barney went up.

And we students made our own decision. Somehow we didn't understand that it was a sign of a disturbed personality. Yes. Because after he called out, he stood and burst out with a wild laugh. His name was R——.

I'm telling you this because of Barney, who—and he became the gabe then. Incidentally, since I already mentioned R——, he later died in an institution for the insane. His psychosis grew worse. He suffered from schizophrenia, and he grew worse and worse. So it turned out that they sent him to some institution and he died there, in the institution.

Anyway, by the time of the incident with the sign regarding the schedule of prayer services, Barney was in his position. I ran over to Barney, and Barney said to me, *"Orders from the boss."* Since I was very, very friendly with Revel—he always stopped when he saw me—I went in to Revel, and said, "Revel," I said, "is it true that you gave an order that on the board notices should be written in English, and not in Yiddish, in our language?"

He said, "Yes." He said, "You must understand, people come

5. More than sixty members of the Jewish community in Hebron were massacred in an attack by local Arab residents in the summer of 1929.

in from California, from everywhere, and it's not fitting that they should see something so prominently [written] on the blackboard, and they don't know what it is."

I said to him, "First of all, Dr. Revel, the people who come from California and from Texas, they know what *Zman tefilas shakhris* means, just as well as they know what it means in English."

He said to me, "Sit down, Noble." He used to call me Noble, as people do in America—Noble. "Noble, sit down." And he said to me, "You know, Noble," he said, "we're in America."

I said, "Yes, I know that very well, and that's why I came to the yeshiva. Because I didn't want to be 'in America.' I wanted somehow to be a little bit more than America, different from America. And based on what that young man from Chicago told me, I thought it was actually a bit different from America here."

And he started working on me: "You don't understand, you don't know America yet, you have to accommodate yourself . . ."

I said, "Ah ha. 'Accommodation' again?" And—I discussed the matter with him a long time, I tried to demonstrate—"Dr. Revel, *zman tefilas minkhe* has a tradition which is probably several hundred years old. Hundreds of years. But this has no tradition. What does it mean? It doesn't say anything. Emotionally it doesn't say anything to me," and so forth. "Morning prayers." Nu—what shall I tell you, children? Who had his way? Of course, Revel. What did I have, me against Revel? And that's how it remained— "Morning prayer, evening prayer." I was very disturbed over this.

At that time I would occasionally study too much. I would get very tired, so I used to take long, long walks. From East Broadway, let's say, I'd walk to 42nd Street, the Fifth Avenue library, that long. Once I passed a church called St. Bartholomew's, very, very . . . And there I saw written on the board, "Vespers."

The word "vespers" really struck my fancy. "Vespers" sounds better than "Evening service."

In short, I came home and took a look, and the announcement still read, "Evening service."

I took a piece of chalk out of my pocket, drew a line through the words "Evening service," and I wrote above it in large letters, "Vespers." Nu—soon Revel walked by, a bit later. And he took a look— "Vespers." He grew angry. And he went straight to me. I was alone in my room, doing my work. And he [knocks], and said, "May I come in?" He spoke to me English, only English, no Yiddish, he never spoke Yiddish. I invited him in, and he said to me, "What did you do, writing 'Vespers'?"

You know, in Yiddish there's a saying—"If you eat pork . . ."

SN, CN, JB: ". . . you might as well go the whole hog."[6]

SN: If it's going to be Goyish, it might as well be a proper Goyish—"Vespers." It sounds much better than the old, coarse "Evening service."

And he grew very, very angry. It was terrible. His face grew red, and he said, "Don't you dare write on the board again."

I saw later that he was a very pious Jew, Revel, a remarkable scholar, had a great deal of learning, but culturally he was an assimilator. And he actually said that to me, he said, "We want it to be in America the way it was in Frankfurt-am-Main." You know what the Jewish community in Frankfurt-am-Main was?

JB: Neo-Orthodoxy.

CN: Breuer.[7]

6. The original Yiddish is "*Az m'est khazer, zol es rinen fun der morde*"—If you're going to eat pork, it should drip off your chin; i.e., if you're sinning already, you might as well do it thoroughly.

7. The reference is to the German Orthodox community founded in Frankfurt-am-Main by Rabbi Samson Raphael Hirsch. It is centered today in Washington Heights, upper Manhattan, and known as the Breuer Community after one of its rabbinical leaders.

SN: Very Orthodox. "That's how we want it," he said.

I said, "I think that's a very big mistake. Our students . . ." But who would listen to me against Revel? Revel was a force. I don't know if you're aware that Revel's father-in-law was a wealthy Jew, one of the first Jewish millionaires. He built Tulsa, Oklahoma, the Jewish community in Tulsa. His father-in-law's name was—Marvis or Parvis, I don't remember, Marvis . . . He came to America and was a peddler here in New York. He wasn't successful. He went off to Oklahoma before it became a state, when it was still a territory. He settled there. Peddled, made a bit of money, and invested in land. Continued peddling, continued investing in land. He bought up a great deal of land. Later, what do you think they suddenly found all over his land?

JB: Oil.

SN: Oil, and he became a Jewish millionaire. And he built up Tulsa, Oklahoma. So, since Revel's father-in-law, one of the richest Orthodox Jews in America at that time, stood behind him, he was a power. If he threatened to leave the yeshiva, people grew scared. The end of the yeshiva! And he was in fact a good organizer as well, apart from his tendency toward assimilation, toward cultural assimilation.

Later I became convinced . . . oh. From that time on the relations between us became a bit cooler. He still asked me, he'd stop me, "How are you, Noble?" But I didn't talk to him, I'd go on with my work.

I really didn't have anything to discuss with him anymore. Let there be what there will be on the bulletin board. They wouldn't let me make my own bulletin board.

In the Prison House of Language

SN: A few months later the following happened: It was winter, Hanukkah. I got a letter from a Jew in Beaver Falls, quite a prosperous Jew, and he included a check for five dollars to celebrate Hanukkah. Gannellen, the Jew's name was. I took the five dollars, and I bought books. I loved books. At that time the first translation of Sholem Aleichem's autobiography *From the Fair* came out. The name in Hebrew was *Khaye adam*,[8] the life of a man. What?

JB: His autobiography.

SN: Yes. The translation was done by his son-in-law, Y. D. Berkovitsh. I had five dollars in my pocket, and I remember I ran off to a bookstore on Canal Street, and I bought two books. One was Sholem Aleichem's translation, wonderful, I got such pleasure from that translation, and the second work was a Hebrew translation of *Ivanhoe*, Scott's *Ivanhoe*. You'll ask me what the connection between those two was, Sholem Aleichem and Scott? We had a . . . yes. Now I have to say a word or two of explanation.

I studied in high school. I began high school. The high school was the worst high school you can imagine. I told you once, for example, that I studied in a bad school in Beaver Falls. That school was so backward that we learned with *McGuffey's Reader*. And did I tell you how we learned spelling, orthography there?

JB: No.

SN: We had a speller. And in that speller there were words, and a mnemonic for the words—for example, *preface: Peter Reilly eats fish and catches eels*. And if the teacher would call out: "Solomon, preface!" I had to answer: "Peter Reilly eats fish and

---

8. This was earlier used as the title of a religious book by Reb Avrom Danzig, a standard guide to everday Jewish law. Thus the parodic borrowing of the title also signifies the transition from standards applicable to any Jew on one hand, to the biographies of distinctive individuals on the other.

catches eels." And for every word there was this kind of mnemonic sentence. A sentence per word, yes. That's how we learned spelling there.

When I entered the yeshiva, I figured it must be more modern—it was much worse. No, it wasn't modern. Let me explain it: The teachers in the yeshiva were also teachers in high school in New York. They would come when school ended. They were supposed to come at three-thirty. But they never did. They all came late. Let's say a teacher taught at DeWitt Clinton High School. How could he arrive on time, even if he left early? So they used to come late. They simply cheated. The yeshiva cheated. We were supposed to have five periods each day. And these were supposed to be between three-thirty and seven. That is, three and a half hours. In a public high school, a period is how much? Ours were forty minutes. The cheating went on in every possible way. We concentrated on the religious subjects, on the Gemore, and the others.

In the first year in high school we read *Ivanhoe*, Scott's *Ivanhoe*. And it took me a year and a day, simply because I didn't know those words. You know, it took me a very long time until I understood the vocabulary from the nineteenth century. We had a bad teacher. So I went and got the Hebrew translation of *Ivanhoe*.

What was the assignment? He said, "Now read from page 12 to page 16 and bring in a summary." I read the book in Hebrew, read it over several times until I'd almost memorized it, and wrote the summaries from the Hebrew text, not from the English. Steinberg was the teacher's name; he was amazed. Steinberg said, "How come the summaries you can write, and when I ask you to read in class. . . ?"

But—the English, I don't know until the present day, children, how we managed to learn anything there. Really, still I don't know. Let me give you an example of the way we learned English. This was in the third year already. In the third year we read a book, Louis Untermeyer's anthology of British poets. Every day we had to read a poem, and write a composition about it for homework. I remember one time a young man stood up, older, he was probably about five or six years older than me, his name was Rabbi Halpern, and he read his composition. The day before we had read "My heart's in the Highlands, my heart is not here, /My heart's"—That's Burns, yes?

CN: Burns, yes.

SN: "My heart's in the Highlands, a-chasing the deer"; and so forth.
   He began his composition this way: "Since he said in the first sentence, 'My heart's in the highlands,' don't I know 'my heart is not here'?" [All laugh.] You understand what that is—it's a Talmudic syllogism. And he developed an entire theme about the significance of this. What the meaning of "My heart's in the Highlands, my heart is not here" is.
   And he carried forth with a long composition, you know, "In the next—I cannot finish, I have no time to finish. And the next I shall tell you in my comp., in my next comp." Composition. He abbreviated it that way: comp.
   That's how we learned. And I remember when we learned Keats: "A thing of beauty is a treasure forever."

CN, JB: "A joy forever."

SN: "A joy forever." And I learned with a boy named Kean, later he became a doctor. He died a few years ago. [Sings to the melody of the first blessing before the Haftorah:] "A thing of beauty is a joy forever." With that sort of melody, so that he would remember it. I tell you, it was bad. I don't know to the present day, maybe you can tell me. But in the end, in the examinations, we all passed the Regents.[9] We learned nothing. But really nothing.

Now there was another factor as well. I told you that I only knew *Ivanhoe* in Hebrew, but I wrote the compositions in English. We were told to write about the action in a particular part. I took a look in the book to see what had happened—the pages were almost the same in Hebrew and in English—found everything out and wrote, Rowena, Rowena is in this scene, and so forth. And he was surprised because when he asked me to read aloud in class, I couldn't do it. "How is it," he asked, "that you write the compositions correctly, but now . . ."

Incidentally this Steinberg also later died in an insane asylum. I remember that Steinberg was a very talented person. He really didn't belong in the yeshiva. He had a Ph.D. from Johns Hopkins. He was an unhappy person. A very decent person . . . Once he told me to read. We had to read two or three books each semester, "outside reading" it was called. He told me to read Joseph Conrad.

Conrad writes about the ocean. I began, and I didn't understand a single word: *fo'c'sle*, and *midriff*,[10] and you know *aft*, the whole terminology. What did I know about it? I'd never even heard of such things. And I told him. And he wanted me to complete it in a certain time, and I said, "Dr. Steinberg, I'm sorry, I just cannot make it in this brief time."

He said, "Why?"

I said, "I have to look—I have to look up every second word."

He said, "Ah, you're looking up words?" He said, "Didn't you guess at it from the context? Nobody looks up every word. You know—guess at it from the context."

SN: I've told you that I entered the yeshiva, yes, and that I had my problems there. I've told you how I wrote on the board—

9. A standardized New York statewide exam for high school students.
10. Presumably Noble means "amidships."

CN: "Vespers."

JB: I told the story to a friend of mine, and he said that his father, who lives on Long Island, became so impatient at a meeting in his synagogue that he said, "People in this temple are so damn couth we ought to say 'vespers' instead of 'evening services.'"

SN: Yes, yes, *couth*. Two things I want to tell you. First of all, I've told you I read the Hebrew translation of Sholem Aleichem's autobiography. I read the book perhaps fifteen times. And every time I found a new flavor in it, it was so—

JB: Why in Hebrew rather than Yiddish?

SN: Why? Oh, I read it in Yiddish as well. Yes, I read it in Yiddish first. But I wanted to see that precious nuance in Hebrew, how he was successful in making it come out as if Sholom Aleichem spoke Hebrew. Wonderful. I carried it with me all the time. Wherever I went, I carried it with me, and whenever I had a free minute, I stole a glance at it. Once as I was walking through the corridor Revel said to me, "Take that book out from under your arm." He took a look, and gave it back to me, and said that he was dissatisfied. "It would be better," he said, "for you to read Dickens."

I was really shocked. Very, very shocked. It was as much of a shock to me as if you would say to me, "It would be better if you converted to Christianity." And I said to him, "I'd like to speak to you about this, Doctor. For me this isn't something to be discussed in one minute, and I want to talk to you about it. I will come to your office, when you have time."

And I said to him the following, I remember very well, because I had prepared: "Dr. Revel, in theory and in principle I am here in order to become a rabbi among Jews, no? That is my task, that is my assignment here. In order to become a rabbi, I have to understand every aspect of Jewish life. Jewish history, Jews, Judaism. And where will I get a better perspective on Jewish life: from Sholem Aleichem, or from Dickens? And on the other hand," I said, "What will Dickens teach me? He'll teach me how Fagin, the thief, teaches children how to be thieves. While Sholem Aleichem teaches me to see all of Jewish life in a different light."

He had no answer to that. And when one feels pressed against the wall, what happens? One becomes angry. His face became red, and he didn't answer at all. Just—yes, I also said the following: "Incidentally, you think I'll learn English from it? I want to tell you the whole truth, Dr. Revel. I long ago gave up the idea that I would learn English here."

And it's like this—I want to tell you parenthetically, that English studies were [inaudible]. There were constantly complaints, for example, to the Board of Education and to Albany that English wasn't taught to us. We were all children of immigrants, you understand. And we all spoke Yiddish. And the little bit that was left for English was truly sorry. Once there was a severe complaint: Most of all our pronunciation was terrible. Someone said that he had come and talked to one of the boys, and he thought that the boy had come from Europe. He asked him, and the boy said no, that he had been born here. So it was decided that we would study elocution. They decided to take away one hour from the English studies one day a week; four hours would be as they were, and the fifth hour would be devoted to elocution.

I'll tell you what elocution was. The teacher was first-class. His name was Lieberman. Perhaps you know—Elias Lieberman was a principal here, he was a poet, he wrote—he [the elocution teacher] was his brother. He didn't have any system. His goal was simply to teach Jews who spoke a bizarre English to speak in a way that could be understood outside New York. The first time

he came in, he said: "I am going to teach you to speak dis-
tinc-tive-ly." And whenever he said dis-*tinc*-tive-ly, he always
grabbed his nose. You understand?

We worked with pairs of sounds. We had particular difficulties
with *v-w*. All immigrant children had difficulties. The voiceless
and the voiced *th*. You know—*this*, *that*, you know. And other
similar things—*r*. With *r* we had very great difficulties. He introduced the following system: He gave us an assignment, let's say,
for the following Friday, "When I call out your name, you are
to give me a sentence which has, let's say, three or four opposi-
tions."

Well, to make a long story short, one time he called on a boy
whose name was Goldberg. I remember him very well. Goldberg
had a weakness: since I knew him, he had been hoarse. It had
something to do with his heart. He called on Goldberg, and that
day we had *v-w*, the opposition *v-w*.

Goldberg got up and read like this: [slow and hoarse] "Every
Vensday evening I take out my goilfriend and I vo her." You
know what "vo her" is?

JB: "Woo her."

SN: "I woo her." "And I vo her." Everybody broke out laughing. He had already sat down. People broke out laughing. When
he saw that people were laughing, he said, "Excuse me, I am a
little hoarse today."

There was Marcus—Marcus Spitz, who later became vice
president of the American Jewish Congress. He got up and said,
"Don't worry, someday you'll grow up to be a big horse!"

And that's what elocution consisted of. That's how they
taught. Yes.

JB: I have a question. It appears to me that very early in your
life, you displayed three characteristics. First, that you had quite
a bit of nerve.

SN: Perhaps then, yes.

JB: You opposed Revel.

SN: At that time, yes.

JB: And second, that you were interested in ethnography, Jewish ethnography. You already had the notion that from Sholem Aleichem one can learn about Jewish lifeways.

SN: I understood that.

JB: And that that is important for a—

SN: For an educated Jew.

JB: And third, linguistics.

SN: Yes, always linguistics. Always interested in linguistics.

JB: It's interesting. Do you have thoughts on where these characteristics, these interests came from?

SN: Oh. My grandfather was quite a researcher of grammar, a remarkable researcher of grammar. Parenthetically, I want to tell you something. Once I was studying with a teacher, with whom I studied Bible; I was a little boy. And this teacher—there's a difficult Rashi, there's a difficult Rashi in the portion *Beshalakh*.[11] In *Beshalakh* there's a very difficult Rashi. Rashi explains a certain difficult point in grammar. And the teacher, Pinyele Melamed, was teaching us this very difficult point. And meanwhile someone, I don't know, some learned Jew came in,

11. In Rashi's commentary on Exodus 15:2.

and says, "Listen, Pinyele. Why are you tormenting the minds of these small children? Can a child understand that?"

He said, "Yes. There is the one boy who will understand." He said, "Shloymele, explain the Rashi."

I began reading back the Rashi, and he was amazed, and he said, "Where do you know so much grammar from?"

I said, "I look at the *Shaarey toyre* together with my grandfather." That's by Reb Zalmen Hanau, from the eighteenth century. A very, very good grammar.

And so much for—yes. I want to tell you the epilogue to this story.

Revel became angry. I saw it clearly. He barely said hello to me when he passed me. And he began explicitly to engage in chicanery against me. What kind of chicanery? I was out in the street, and I was eating an apple. You'd think it's nothing, probably you, too, ate an apple in the street when you were in school. Revel came up and said, "Noble, go in and look at the tractate of *Kedushin*[12] in the Talmud, page so-and-so."

I became afraid: "What's this about?" I came home and ran and grabbed the tractate *Kedushin*, and took a look: *Haokhel bashuk dome lekelev.*[13] "Whoever eats in the street is just like a dog." I resented it. After all, was I the only one who . . . A lot of young people eat while they're walking in the street. I was simply hungry.

And he began causing problems for me. Once he came to me. I lived there, I had a room there, and he came into my room. He and two others came in and looked over the books I had on my shelves. They looked over all my books. I actually had a book that might have really drawn his attention. I had Markish's *The Heap.*[14] Have you ever read Markish's *The Heap*? He describes

12. The tractate dealing primarily with betrothals.
13. *Kedushin* 40:B.
14. The poet Peretz Markish was one of the Yiddish cultural leaders killed by Stalin in 1952.

the experiences of the destruction of Jewish life during the Ukrainian pogroms. But that he didn't pay attention to. What drew his attention was Shneour's poems—I had Shneour there in Hebrew, I had Hebrew and Yiddish together. Shneour had a Hebrew poem there called "Romance." But he didn't say anything about it, and I didn't say anything about the fact that he had come to look over my books. How did I know? The janitor was a Pole from our neighborhood in Galicia, and I became acquainted with him, and he often did me favors, he gave me an extra towel or an extra pillow to sleep on.

Besides that—for example, we published a Hebrew journal, the students, it was hectographed. It was called *Yavne*. It's very rare; probably there are still somewhere copies of *Yavne*. I was one of the editors. The other was Ben Zion—Ben Zion Bokser.[15] He was the second. And the third was a boy who left Jewish life entirely—Raderzhinsky. Yes. Later he distanced himself from Jewish life. Became a rich man, this Raderzhinsky, but he left Jewish life.

For each issue—four times a year—for each issue I had to go get permission. I said, "Whoever heard of such a thing, having to go for each issue of a journal?"

No, he wanted me to come show him the material. Good. I came, and showed him the material. And he hesitated often: "Perhaps this is not necessary, we don't need that."

Growing Doubts

SN: I'll tell you, I already began to think at that time, "Somehow this isn't for me. Somehow this isn't for me."

Incidentally there was something earlier, that I hadn't experi-

15. 1907–1984. Conservative rabbinical leader, author and professor at Jewish Theological Seminary.

enced, which my father described to me. My father arrived from Europe, and he was looking for a job in New York. Just then my grandfather died. My father was saying Kaddish, and every day he prayed in the same synagogue, three times a day. There he became acquainted with a certain Jew by the name of ——. And this —— became friendly, very friendly with my father. One day —— asked him: "Mr. Noble, what is your occupation?"

My father said, "I'm looking for a position."

He said, "Good. Do you know what I have for you? This job is just right for you. I have a sausage factory, a kosher sausage factory in ——. It's not hard work, but you have to get up early. You have to—the work begins five, six o'clock in the morning, and you'll have to be there before the meat arrives."

My father said, "I get up early anyway."

And they agreed. And he told him that the salary was very good: forty dollars a week. In those days, forty dollars was a massive amount of money.

And my father accepted. It was a Sunday. It was a Sunday—because they worked on Sunday there. My father set out for his new job. And he arrived there, before they started work, of course. He stood and watched. Soon the manager arrived, the foreman, and opened up. And he sees there's a Jew standing there, "What do you want, sir?" he asked.

My father said, "I'm the new *mashgiach*."[16]

He said, "Come in. Mr. Mashgiach, let me tell you something. Do what the previous mashgiach did. Come in Friday, take your check with you, and go in health. And don't show up during the entire week. That's what the previous mashgiach did, and you should do the same thing. And Friday your check will be waiting for you here."

"That's how it is?" My father said. "Find yourself another mashgiach." That was it for him as a mashgiach. My father came home, and that was it for him as a mashgiach.

16. The kashrut supervisor.

My father told me the story, and I began thinking to myself, "That's what Jewish life in America is like? That's how it is? When they hire a mashgiach, they tell him, 'Be our guest, stay at home. Come Friday and pick up your check.'"

And thus I began to have doubts about Jewish life in America. And there were other episodes.

The uncle with whom I had once lived was involved in a legal dispute adjudicated by a rabbi named Gudzhik. The case had to do with a mutual aid society which had split, and there was a question concerning the society's cemetery plot, how were they going to divide the cemetery plot, and so forth. He was always involved in legal disputes. He was always in a civil court or a rabbinical court.

Gudzhik lived on Attorney Street, Rabbi Gudzhik, and my uncle told me that he gone to him in connection with a case, and he had lost the case. He lost the case, and as he was talking with Gudzhik, Gudzhik said, "You know, if you give me fifty dollars . . ." My uncle took it out and gave him—I don't know how much, I don't remember exactly how much. Rabbi Gudzhik ran to the door and shouted to the other party, who had already gone downstairs, "Oh, there's new evidence! There's new evidence! The case is reopened! Come back, come back!" New evidence—the new evidence was what?

JB: The dollars.

SN: The fifty dollars he gave him.

I began to have a rather negative view of America. "Why do I need to get involved in it? I'll become a rabbi, and they'll give me the fifty dollars, I'll be the one who takes it . . ." I decided that I wouldn't go into the rabbinate. That was the beginning of 1924. Early 1924, that's when the crisis came. From 1921—24. I already had had three years of high school. And—of course, I announced it to my father, and I told him it wasn't for me. My father said, "Well, all right, if it won't be that, find yourself something else. Find yourself something else."

During the three years, I had accumulated fifteen Regents points—you know what that is, and in order to enter college you had to have sixteen. So I didn't really need the fourth year. I decided—I don't know how it happened, I decided to go to Johns Hopkins. It took my fancy. I inquired, and they answered positively, that they would accept me on condition that I would make up intermediate algebra.

But there are a few things I want to tell you about before we leave the yeshiva for good.

I learned a lot. I learned a lot. I had one teacher who simply fell in love with me, Rabbi Levine was his name. And he simply didn't want to let me go away. I had to stay with him, and stay and stay and stay . . . and he even thought that I had many other talents in addition to learning. Once he asked me to come to his house. Something was wrong with the radiator. He wanted me to fix it. "Ah," he said, "where there is Torah, there is also competence." I came, and I spent an entire Sunday, and of course I couldn't fix it. He sat there sitting very sadly. Not because I couldn't fix it, but—"I must have overestimated you a bit. Since you studied so well, I thought you could do this as well. You mustn't be quite as much of a student as I thought."

Nothing. That's how it was. Suddenly I decided that I had altogether lost my desire for learning. And Levine even noticed that I wasn't studying enthusiastically. "Oh," he said, "I know why you've lost your enthusiasm for learning." I simply didn't want to tell a lie. "You know, there's a verse in Psalms— *Amar naval belibo—eyn elohim.*"[17] "The fool said in his heart, 'There is no God.' " Once he looked at me, and he said, "I know why you've lost your enthusiasm for learning. *Amar Noble belibo—* this fellow Noble thinks in his heart, *eyn elohim,* that there is no God."

17. Psalms 14:1.

There was a bit of truth in that. I began to have some hereti-
cal thoughts. But on the other hand, I began to read a great deal
at that time. I got hold of a novel which was very popular at
that time. It was Sinclair Lewis's *Main Street*.[18] That book really
caused a revolution in America. A revolution in American
thought. And somewhere I got hold of *Main Street*. And I began
reading it, and read it with intense . . . You've probably all read
Main Street, no? But you know what it is. It's simply a satire of,
so to speak, bourgeois, small-town life in America. It made a
powerful impression.

I began to be very interested in theater at that time. Somehow
the American theater—of course, I had no money to go, but I
read, you know, the press, the reviews, sometimes a book. At
that time I came across a new figure in American drama—
Eugene O'Neill. I read Eugene O'Neill, and I was simply captivated. Captivated.

Incidentally, at the same time I began to find the life in the
yeshiva, let's say, very narrow, very oppressive. There were
things we didn't have, that were lacking. Yes, true, I sat and
studied in the shtetl—I had or I didn't have—but now I began
to resent these things.

For example, once they decided that during the winter, at ten
o'clock the lights go out. Everyone had to be in bed at ten
o'clock. That was when I still had my crowd. The students asked
me to go talk to Revel. They thought I still had good relations
with Revel. I said, "No, I won't talk to Revel. We'll do what
everybody does. We'll go to bed at ten o'clock. What can we
do?" That was the decision: at ten o'clock we would go to bed.

I lived on the second floor. Once I came from the third on a
Friday night, when it was dark. I came down from the third
floor; I had seen a student there. It was like this: one flight of
stairs here, and then a landing, and then another flight. From

18. Published in 1920.

these stairs, the second stairs, I jumped. Jumped down, and landed in front of my door. When I got down in front of my door, I saw that the light in my room had gone on. "Oh," I said. And it burned all night, all that Sabbath. Apparently I had jarred something when I jumped. The electric wiring was old, the building was God knows how old, when I jumped down something moved, and my light went on . . .

When others jumped, they didn't find the board. It was only if you jumped on that particular board that the light went on. And I became somewhat of a celebrity among the students. They began asking me, "Go up and jump." And all the students were there in my room—I don't know, five, six, eight—we were sitting there, you know, chatting, telling stories, I don't know what. One time Rabbi Altshuler came by. He was one of the three who had been in my room to inspect. And he noticed that the whole building was dark, but there was a light on in one room. My room faced the street, East Broadway. He went to the janitor, and—"What's going on?"

He said, "I don't know. I pulled the switch. I don't know how—"

Altshuler came to speak to me. He wanted me to tell him the secret of how I turned the light on. "That's a secret," I said, "between me and the Lord of the Universe. I can't tell anyone else. Only the Lord knows, and I know. Others will never know."

They threatened to fire the janitor. They said it had to be some sort of conspiracy between me and the janitor. "How did you—"

He swore. He said, "So help me God, I don't know a thing. Maybe he has a key."

They begged me and begged me, they even promised to give me things. "No, I won't tell." And that's how it remained. And they decided that they'd leave the lights on in the entire building. Because if I could turn lights on . . . And thus I averted the evil decree that everyone had to be in bed asleep at ten o'clock.

What else did I want to tell you about the yeshiva? Oh. This will interest you. In the yeshiva, girls were taboo. They literally, physically, didn't allow any girls into the yeshiva. Whenever they saw a girl, they interrogated her. They asked her whom she was coming to see, whom she wanted to see, and she wouldn't be allowed to go into the rooms. And she stood downstairs, and everyone walked by and looked at her . . . In general, there was a view of girls or women that was really bizarre. I called it the monasticism of the yeshiva. Meanwhile we were young people, you know, there were students who were a bit older. And when we saw a girl, we would simply faint. When a girl came in on Sunday, let's say, people came running to look at her. "What does this creature look like? Does it look like a person or like a goose?"

I only had one encounter with a girl at the yeshiva. On Passover of 1924, my father got a temporary job in Knoxville, Tennessee.[19] He left for Knoxville, Tennessee, before Passover. And we decided that I would go to be with him on Passover in Knoxville, Tennessee. In those years my father was not at all worldly, and we both thought that the ticket to Knoxville, Tennessee, would be four or five dollars. When we went to buy a ticket, they told me it would be nearly twenty dollars a ticket at that time to Knoxville, Tennessee. I didn't even dream of having that much money. In short, I remained in New York for Passover. Meanwhile, no one had invited me for Passover, the way people usually invited the students, because I had said I was going home. Here it was just before Passover, and I didn't have anywhere to spend the holiday

To make a long story short, a Jew by the name of Krim came

19. Smaller Jewish communities, particularly in rural areas, frequently hire a qualified person to serve as visiting rabbi on major holidays such as Passover or the High Holidays.

to me. Peyskeh Krim was the Jew's name. He was a vice president of the Borden Company and he wanted me to be a *mashgiach* at the Borden Company for Passover, somewhere in upstate New York, to be a mashgiach supervising the milking of the cows. There wasn't a single Jew in that place. "What will I eat?"

"You'll have matzos, eggs, hard-boiled eggs." I refused. I didn't go.

Passover approached. And on the last day a Jew came in, and his name was Sirota. And this Jew Sirota said, "You haven't been invited anywhere?"

I said, "I don't have anywhere to go for the seder."

He said, "Come to me."

And I went to him, to Sirota. He was a simple Jew, a baker. I had a fine Passover. But the noteworthy thing was that there was a girl there, more or less my age. It was the first time I saw that a girl is a creature like all human beings—she has arms, she has feet. And there was more. The girl studied in *Bet sefer leumi*, which was a very good Hebrew school at that time. She was, I think, a year younger than me. And we had a very good time. Spent the first two days of Passover, and they asked me to come for the intermediate days as well, and I went, but not the whole time.

The girl was very lively. Very, very vivacious. Not withdrawn at all. I don't know—one time she took a notion into her head. Somehow she stole into the yeshiva. The girl came into the yeshiva. I wasn't in my room. I was in the class where we studied Gemore. And she even found out where my room was. She came into my room, and left a note. She left a piece of paper, and on it was written in large letters: *"Ve'im lo akhshav, aymatay?"*[20] You know what that is?

20. Noble pronounced this phrase according to the modern Hebrew system used by the Zionists, which would have been taught at the *Bet sefer leumi*, rather than as traditional Ashkenazic Hebrew, which would have been in use at the Yeshiva Isaac Elhanan.

JB: Do you understand?

CN: No, no.

JB: "If not now, when?"[21]

SN: If not now, when then? There it was in large letters on the paper. I came in. I recognized her handwriting. She had a sort of ornamental handwriting, with curlicues. I had helped her with her compositions. She knew a good deal of Hebrew, but not too much. For a high school girl in those times it was average, today it would be too much for a rabbi. And I sat there: *Im lo akhshav, aymatay.* It was clear that it was a girl's handwriting. A female's handwriting is discernible. And I thought to myself: What could it mean? In addition I began to think: Perhaps someone else saw this? It could be that someone from the administration had come, and seen it. *Im lo akhshav aymatay?* They would bring me in to be questioned, there would have been a real inquisition. You know what an inquisition is? "Who wrote this? How did the girl get in? After all, we're so careful." There was an attic, and I went up there. I sat down and wrote this: "Now is the time for us to give our children a real Jewish education." I began with "Everything is lost now . . ." and I wrote a long essay, you know, as if it were an article for our journal. "Now is the time . . ." and the headline, you know, is very appropriate, very appropriate: "If not now, when?"

And I left it on the table. And other boys came, and they read it. "Oh, that's quite . . . What's this article? Who wrote it?"

"I'll tell you," I said. Since only students in the yeshiva wrote, I said that one of the students had written it, but the headline was written by his sister. It worked. I didn't have any difficulties.

21. This is the conclusion of the famous saying of Rabbi Hillel: "If I am not for myself, who will be for me? And if I am only for myself, who am I? And if not now, when?" (Mishnah Avot 1:14.)

I didn't think about the issue too much. Somehow I had gotten myself out of the tough spot.

One other time I had difficulties. This time it happened this way: At that time I decided to find out what it was like in another Jewish school. I figured there must be other Jewish schools. The Herzliah. Have you ever heard of the Herzliah? It was a leftist school. The Herzliah had opened at that time, it opened in 1921. The poet Shimen Halprin gave a course there, and I registered for the course in Hebrew literature. And there were many girls there. And in general it was different—a different approach. They didn't use the Talmudic gestures, on the one hand this, and on the other hand that . . . "Since it says in the first sentence 'My heart's in the Highlands,' why does he have to say in the second sentence 'My heart is not here'?"

I enjoyed myself. When Purim came that year, Herzliah published a humorous journal. The journal was called *Laglag*. An invented name, *Laglag*, "mocked." They asked me to write something. At that time I had just gone for an interview. They needed a Hebrew teacher somewhere. They wrote, "We're looking for a Hebrew teacher, cheap." At the interview, they asked me, "Do you know this? Do you know that? Bible?"

And to everything I responded, "Yes."

Afterward they asked me, "Can you sing?"

I said, "Well, I'm not a Metropolitan Opera star. But . . ." In short, I didn't get the position.

Oh yes—they asked me, "Are you religious?"

I thought—and I included this in what I wrote— "Perhaps I should say yes. *Meyle, tehey da'as*—let there be religion, *bilvad shetehey parnose*—as long as I can earn a living." That's what I wrote. In short, that came out in *Laglag*. There was a student in the yeshiva who was a son of Y. Z. Frishberg. The father was an old Hebrew teacher here, very respected. His son was Naftoli, he's already dead, Naftoli. Naftoli had to write a composition for the yeshiva, so he copied from *Laglag* the article I had written there. But he didn't understand everything that he copied. In the yeshiva they saw that: "Let there be religion, as long as there's livelihood"—that's not Orthodox thinking! What's this—"Let there be religion, as long as there's religion!" And they called Naftoli Frishberg out on the carpet in the yeshiva. He admitted that he had copied it, and the one who had written it was Shloyme Noble.

"Shloyme Noble! Oh!" That was precisely what the administration needed. In short, they called me in to explain: "What does this mean?"

I said, "That was for Purim, after all." I wanted to make up an excuse. "Purim, you have to get drunk. According to Jewish law you have to get drunk on Purim. This isn't something serious. What are you taking it seriously for? Who takes seriously something that was written for Purim?" I babbled about Purim. I barely got myself out of it.

But the last blow I felt came when we had high school examinations in 1924. We had a principal in the high school by the name of Safire. He was a brutal person, you can't imagine. Really, a sadist. During the Regents Exam Safire came in for some reason, while the students were sitting and writing.

And there was a boy named Morgenstern. And suddenly he walked up and took Morgenstern's paper, "Morgenstern, you copied! You looked at your neighbor's paper!"

Morgenstern said, "No." He began defending himself—

He said, "Why did you have your eyes off your paper?"

He said, "You get tired when you sit two hours, you know." How much—two hours or more, how much is a Regents Examination?

CN: It takes two hours in theory, but it takes a much shorter time, a half hour or an hour.

SN: Yes. He said, "I'm sitting here for so long, that my head hurt from just looking at this piece of paper. I lifted my head," he said.

In short, he didn't want to hear about it. Morgenstern was a senior. He had to graduate that year. He tore his paper. Morgenstern began to cry, and he asked, "Will I graduate?"

He answered, "No, you'll have to take the course again." And so forth.

And I resented that bitterly. I resented that very, very bitterly. I thought that Morgenstern had been brutally treated. But classes were still going on. I don't know how that could have been. Morgenstern committed a folly. A somewhat twisted boy he was, that Morgenstern. He took revenge on Safire in a very childish way. He stole into Safire's room and took revenge on his desk. And the result was that Safire called police into the building, and the police took the boy, Morgenstern, away.

I saw this and I said, "Shloyme, time to pack your things and run away. Get yourself out of here." That's how it ended.

COMMENTARY

The young Shlomo Noble considered the Rabbi Isaac Elhanan Yeshiva to be a failed attempt at cultural synthesis, and this chapter
details the various aspects of that failure. Through these episodes
the figure of Noble as trickster comes forth more clearly than in
the previous chapters, as he becomes more and more aware that
the Orthodox institutional framework is not for him.

Like the previous chapter, this one begins with a memory of an
event in the annual cycle, here Passover instead of Thanksgiving.
But rather than the shining Seder table, what Noble recalls is the
dirt and confusion of the frenzied spring cleaning done just before
the holiday. This opening visual scene of disorder stands out in a
narrative where almost all of the conflicts have to do with disorders
of language.

Also like the previous chapter, Noble grounds this one in a reference to popular culture which we are able to share. The figure of
Joe Namath stood as guarantor that Beaver Falls was not merely a
fictional town, without invading Noble's narrative in any way.
Here the song and cartoon character Barney Google, while serving
to connect Noble's audience to the setting of his tale, displaces the
traditional Jewish ritual forms of respectful address with disastrous
consequences. It is not only the young man himself who is mocked;
by having him publicly addressed as *ben moreynu Reb Google*, the
son of Reb Google, his genealogy is also denied him. In retelling
the story, Noble comes very close to joining in with the disturbed
young man who so insulted Barnett, when he refers to Barnett as
"Barney Goo—." Likewise, Noble attempts to rebuke Charles and
me for laughing at this anecdote, and then laughs himself.

The real disaster in this situation, of course, happened not to
Barnett but to the perpetrator, who failed to recognize the accept-
able boundaries of linguistic play. Sometimes Trickster loses his
moorings, steps beyond the bounds of what the community will
tolerate, cannot appropriately handle the chasm between culture
and situation. Noble tells us that after causing Barnett public
shame, this young "eternal student" who has been through all the

yeshivas in Lithuania ultimately dies in an insane asylum. While Noble emphasizes that the yeshiva was intended as a model of how American and Orthodox Jewish cultural models could be synthesized, for this young man, the attempt failed in the most drastic way conceivable. Nor is he the only victim of this type; Steinberg, one of the secular teachers, ends up in the same place. Noble does not directly diagnose either case as culturally induced schizophrenia, but their occurrence within this setting certainly increases the sense of badly managed cultural encounter.

The description of the English language instruction at the yeshiva can be read as a continuation of Khayemke's teaching in Beaver Falls. An attempt is made to master English without leaving the Yiddish and Jewish textual idiom. Thus the analysis of Robert Burns using traditional Talmudic reasoning—which actually seems wonderfully prescient of certain styles in literary theory today—nevertheless suggested to Noble that two cultures can be "synthesized" in a way that makes a mockery of both of them.

Noble does not blame these failures on the ignorance of the students, but on the misplaced values of the yeshiva administration. On one hand, he claims, Bernard Revel believed in a cultural assimilation which to Noble entailed the sacrifice of essential elements of Jewishness, but on the other hand the yeshiva administration was incapable of enabling that assimilation through adequate instruction. Noble's angry retort to the suggestion that he read Dickens rather than Sholem Aleichem reveals a high degree of Jewish pride: if he's to be a leader of Jews, why should he read anti-Semitic literature? On the other hand, the form of literature mattered at least as much as the content. Studying English rather than reading Yiddish or Hebrew was for Noble equivalent to studying Christianity rather than Judaism. Throughout his life he retained this passionate conviction that language is not merely an arbitrary vessel but rather the very embodiment of history. The narrative suggests that for Revel, Sholem Aleichem was not necessarily culturally inferior to Dickens, but more urgently, that Yiddish secular literature was the exact opposite of the American religious Orthodoxy Revel wanted to promote. On the contrary, Noble's preference for Sholem Aleichem doubtless reflects the fact that this beloved author was himself conscious of the need to document and creatively transform the cultural resources of the shtetl.

Noble states as much in defending his transgressive response to Revel's choice of "Evening services" over *Zman tefilas minkhe:*" "Dr. Revel, *zman tefilas minkhe* has a tradition which is probably several hundred years old. Hundreds of years. But this has no tradition." Here Trickster acts to defend the tradition. Decades later, Noble creates a narrative by showing how he protested and sometimes overcame a rigidified set of cultural conventions. It was Trickster as well who discovered how to free his fellow students from Friday night confinement to darkness in their own quarters by turning on a light after the current had been switched off—significantly, in that case it was the very age and quirkiness of the building that made this trick possible. The risks Noble took in criticizing pretensions and impositions from within left him an institutionally marginal man, but a fully human Jew.

Noble's gradual estrangement from Orthodoxy—which began even before he came to America—was stimulated by his own internal debates about knowledge and belief, by disappointment at the intellectual inadequacy of the defenders of the faith, and by confrontation with out-and-out religious corruption. Writing an article for a journal issue set to come out around the time of Purim—when, as discussed in the first chapter, parodic and mildly transgressive versions of traditional discourse were accepted—gave him a chance to express some of his growing perceptions about the gap between professed belief and unprincipled behavior. Unfortunately, the article fell into the wrong hands. The excuse that it was Purim saved him, but the whole experience, rather than offering him a safety outlet for his skepticism, increased his sense of alienation from the yeshiva.

Noble does not make clear what he thought at the time of the practice of isolating the young men at the yeshiva from any contact with young women. In retrospect, it evidently strikes him as an unwarranted impingement on their personal development. The story about the message left for him—"If not now, when?"—

dramatizes the extent of this isolation, through his frantic effort to avoid the terrible threat of discovery. Noble knew that writing could both liberate and cause disaster. The way in which he turns the damning evidence into a laudable piece of conventional exhortation is another demonstration of Trickster's way with language. Beyond that, however, there is a pathos in the contradiction between the urgency of the message—"If not now, when?"—and the ease with which it was turned into a pietistic truism. Rabbi Hillel's statement, which for a character like Noble could apply equally well to romance and to the preservation of a traditional culture, was here betrayed by duplicity.

If Noble had come to the yeshiva to be away from America in America, his enthusiasm too was betrayed. The yeshiva could not shelter him from the rabbinic corruption he'd seen in the small town, nor could it support his devotion to Jewish languages and to the texts written in them, whether religious or secular. For Noble at this stage, greediness for money and the assimilationist spirit were linked to that "higher unity" which his friend Shaber had spoken of, which so shocked him and which was for him the ultimate betrayal of the linked ideals of Jewish tradition and of socialism. Thus when Noble speaks of "a revolution from left to right," he is making a profound pun: the switch from the Hebrew alphabet to the Latin at the same time represented a political abandonment of the millennial, critical force of Jewish memory.

7

The Wandering Scholar

A Year Among the Southern Gentry

SN: I arrived in Baltimore with God's help. What did I do in Baltimore? I had a Bible teacher in the yeshiva[1] named Moyshe Zaydel. He wrote to me that he needed a teacher, and he thought that I would be very appropriate as a teacher in the school. He very much wanted me to come. And just then I was ready to leave, so I said, "Yes, I'll come. I'm actually thinking of going to Johns Hopkins, I've been accepted."

He said, "Good."

So I arrived in Baltimore and became a teacher in Dr. Zaydel's Talmud Torah. It was a very good Talmud Torah. And I was satisfied there.

I worked very, very hard, because I had very good teachers at Johns Hopkins. First-class teachers. I want to tell you about one of them in particular. There was one named French. French taught English. His name was Dr. French, he taught English.

Remember, I told you that I had had a teacher in the yeshiva

1. Evidently this was a teacher at the Yeshiva Isaac Elhanan.

173

who had advised me, "Noble, don't be silly. Don't look up words. Whoever looks up words in a dictionary? You guess from the context."

From that time on I hardly opened a dictionary. Whenever I encountered a word, I guessed at that. With guessing, you're never entirely certain that you understand. I began to write compositions for this Professor French. He always went over them very carefully, improving and pointing things out. One time he called me in and said, "I have the feeling that you're never certain of the words you write. There's an uncertainty, an ambiguity about it." He said, "I would recommend that you should look up every word that you're not certain about. And if not," he said, "I'll ask you. I'll check on it."

And he would ask me. I had written, let's say, "abstruse." He said, "Noble, tell me, what is 'abstruse.'"

And I would cite the dictionary: "Abstruse means 'vague, dark.'"

Later I began to resent it: Was I different from all the other students? The other students were freshmen just like me, weren't they? Why didn't he ask them? Why didn't he ask Trueheart, or Reynolds, or another student, my friends there—he only asks me.

I thought it over: It made no sense to protest. So one time I did the following: I deliberately wrote the word "apocryphal." I went to the O.E.D., the Oxford English Dictionary. And I copied out of the Oxford English Dictionary everything that it says about 'apocryphal.' You know what the Oxford English Dictionary is like . . .

"Noble," he asked me, "What is 'apocryphal'?"

I took out my paper and began to read: "'Apocryphal' is from the Greek 'apokryptein,'" and I read and read, and I saw that the students were sitting there, nodding their heads, falling asleep. And he himself began to fall asleep.

He said to me, "Perhaps that will be enough?"

I said, "No, no, I still have two pages." And I read—and you know what happened? The bell rang, and I still had more to read!

He stopped.

Perhaps you have questions?

JB: Did you encounter anti-Semitism in Johns Hopkins?

SN: No. No. It appeared so to me at that time. There was a professor of classical languages, Latin and Greek. Edwards was his name. Very thin. And we had lockers. You know, in the basement we had lockers. And I had a locker, and next to me there was a Jewish student from New York by the name of Jacobson. You know how it is with lockers—one time Jacobson couldn't get the locker open. He twisted it this way and that way. He was in a hurry. He got a bit nervous, and shouted out, "Jesus Christ!"

Professor Edwards happened to be going by just then. He walked up to him and he said, "Mr. Jacobson"—he knew him, he was a student of his—"Mr. Jacobson, millions of people take this name with great reverence and awe."

I thought this was anti-Semitic, but in later years, the more I think about it, I see that it was just my sensitivity. That wasn't anti-Semitism.

CN: My father taught me the same thing. You can't say "Jesus Christ" because a Gentile might come in and be offended.

JB: I complained to Christian friends in my childhood that they shouldn't shout, "Grandma Moses!" To me it was just like "Jesus Christ!" I didn't know who Grandma Moses was.

SN: But this I must tell you. In Johns Hopkins the spirit at that time was very, very Victorian. They called us "young gentlemen," and so forth. I expected modern ideas there, and—I'll tell you. In 1924 it was a presidential election year. And in 1924 there was a socialist candidate, La Follette.[2] Have you ever heard of La Follette?

CN: Fighting Bob.

SN: Fighting Bob, yes, was running for president then. I came into class with an election button, "Vote for La Follette." There was a Professor Parrish, a frightful reactionary. When he saw the button, he became agitated, and he said, "Even here they're coming in with those buttons?" That is—in Hopkins, the citadel of—

JB: The ivory tower.

SN: Yes, the ivory tower. And he said to me, "Noble, you should have been on the ark, you know, Noah's ark." At that time they were sending back Communists . . . Do I have a bit more time?

Have you ever heard of the Palmer raids? Mitchell Palmer raids? At the beginning of the twenties they seized people and sent them back, Berkman and a woman, what was the woman's name—

JB: Emma Goldman.

SN: Emma Goldman. Yes, Emma Goldman and Berkman. "You should have been on the ark with them."

I looked at him. I said, "What? The American government permits this on its ballot, and here . . ."

2. Robert M. La Follette actually ran under the banner of the League for Progressive Political Action, which was established for the presidential campaign.

He said to me: "I know whose disciple you are. I know whose disciple you are. You're Norman Thomas's disciple."

I said, "What? Is Norman Thomas God? He is a person." From then on I had big problems with that professor, with Parrish. He began to be personally afraid that there was a revolutionary, a Communist sitting there. He began giving me problems. He said that I hadn't given him an assignment, though I had given him the assignment . . .

SN: Today I want to summarize the year in Baltimore. I promised to tell you about an episode that began in 1921 and repeatedly erupted into my life. I'll tell you later; it's about a person whom I'm afraid of till this day. Somehow I'm afraid of him. We'll talk about that. Now I want to talk about Baltimore.

For me it was a very blessed year. In Baltimore I read very, very much English. But I didn't study Gemore anymore. I read a bit of Yiddish, Hebrew, but no more Gemore. I devoted myself entirely to reading English.

In Baltimore I made the acquaintance of V. F. Calverton. Victor Febronius Calverton. Once his name was George Goetz. He was a Jewish boy, regardless of that resonant Anglo-Saxon name Victor Febronius Calverton. He was a Jewish boy, but quite competent. At that point he was publishing *The Modern Quarterly*. Later *The Modern Quarterly* changed, it became *The Modern Monthly*, and I think it's still published today.[3] It was a leftist journal. It was really far to the left. A very talented young man, this Victor Febronius Calverton. He died a long time ago. And I remember that thanks to him I became acquainted there with Sidney Hook. Sidney Hook was writing a series in *The Modern Quarterly* at that time against Communism. He attacked Communism, and Calverton responded. Calverton was pro-Commu-

3. The name was changed to *The Modern Monthly* in 1933 and back to *The Modern Quarterly* in 1938. Publication ceased entirely in 1940.

nist. And Hook was anti-Communist already at that point. Calverton was a Trotskyist.

And in addition there was the one they called the Sage of Baltimore. You know who that was?

CN: Mencken?

SN: Mencken, yes. A fine person he was. A very fine person. And a talented person, extremely talented. Except for—he was a bit of a crank, he did nothing but fight wars against the *"booboisie,"* and you know, with the Establishment he was constantly carrying on a big war.

JB: What contacts did you have with Mencken?

SN: Mencken asked me questions about Yiddish. Mencken was very interested in Yiddish, you know, very interested in Yiddish. Mencken knew German very well. He was from a German family. And I would just compare for him, "German is like this, and Yiddish is like this." And other similar things.

And in addition to his craziness about the *booboisie*, he was antireligious, dreadfully antireligious. I once told him that the next day I was going to pray, it's Yom Kippur. He looked at me and he said, "You still believe in that?"

I said, "Yes."

"Ha," he laughed. He was very, very antireligious.

JB: He was a journalist.

SN: What? He published *The American Mercury*. He was the editor of *The American Mercury* with George Jean Nathan.

And as I've said, we mostly talked about linguistic issues.

He published the series *Prejudices*. You probably know the series *Prejudices*, in which he carried on a war against the Establishment. *Prejudices* came out I believe in six series, six volumes—*Prejudices*, *More Prejudices*, *Still More Prejudices*, and so forth.

He had a very good influence on me.

SN: That was the plus. I really learned a lot of English, I read . . . On the other hand I was immediately disappointed with the university. I sat down to learn English, and I learned English. I sat down to learn, let's say, solid geometry, and I learned solid geometry. But the spirit didn't please me at all. The spirit there, I remember, was Victorian. Altogether Victorian. I expected somehow new thoughts, that I'd hear some new idea, a new approach. No. In those times literature was taught exactly the way it was in the Victorian Era. Just like in the Victorian period.

I met other people and I asked them, "What's it like in . . . "

And they said that Columbia was more liberal. Columbia was already much more liberal at that time. You understand, Hopkins is in Baltimore. And it remained a Southern institution, a school for the Southern gentry. The names of my friends there—Reynolds, Trueheart, Holliday—demonstrate the point. I had no pleasure from that spirit. In addition I saw that they got no pleasure from me. For example—there was a forum, a very good forum. I heard one good lecturer, Walter de la Mare. Have you heard of him?

CN: The poet.

SN: Another time there was a lecture which greatly interested me. It was by a woman who was the principal of the girls' high school in Baltimore, her name was Lizette Woodworth Reese. I read a little bit about her. I took out her book with a piece of poetry. She had one poem which was anthologized, "Tears, Idle Tears."[4] Have you heard of it?

CN: No.

SN: Nothing, it's nothing. Really in the true Victorian spirit. Nu. And she announced a lecture about "Baltimore in American Literature." I prepared myself quite carefully for this lecture. I really expected to hear great things from her, because people recommended her highly . . . She had nothing to say. A very respectable, sweet old lady. But she lived entirely in the nineteenth century. This was in 1924. She began with Sidney Lanier. She spoke a lot about him, and then she moved on to Edgar Allan Poe, who was also in Baltimore. She said a good deal about him. And then she spoke about, you know, local talent. For example, Reverend Albert Muddy who wrote a poem about the dedication of a church, and other similar things, you know, the real amateurs . . . And she finished there.

4. Reese lived from 1856 to 1935 and published several poetical and autobiographical works. "Tears, Idle Tears" is actually the title of a famous poem by Tennyson. Noble was doubtless thinking of Reese's sonnet "Tears," for which she is best known.

> When I consider Life and its few years—
> A wisp of fog betwixt us and the sun;
> A call to battle, and the battle done
> Ere the last echo dies within our ears;
> A rose choked in the grass; an hour of fears;
> The gusts that past a darkening shore do beat;
> The burst of music down an unlistening street—
> I wonder at the idleness of tears.
> Ye old, old dead, and ye of yesternight,
> Chieftains, and bards, and keepers of the sheep,
> By every cup of sorrow that you had,
> Loose me from tears, and make me see aright
> How each hath back what once he stayed to weep;
> Homer his sight, David his little lad!

From *The Selected Poems of Lizette Woodworth Reese*, New York: George H. Doran, 1926. My thanks to Professor Avrom Fleishman of Johns Hopkins University—absolutely no relation to the protagonist of the next chapter—for this reference.

I stood up. I asked a question. I said, "I only know that in addition to those whom you mentioned, there is now being published a journal called *Baltimore Poets*, young poets."

She said, "I've never seen it." She said, "Have you seen it?"

I said, "Yes. In addition I wanted to say that Upton Sinclair is from Baltimore." And he was writing then. "And furthermore there lives in Baltimore, probably a stone's throw from us, H. L. Mencken. He is also an interesting figure, who should at least have been mentioned. And furthermore," I said, "this year's winner of the *Nation* poetry prize" was a young man named Segal—a Jew, of course—who wrote a modern poem called "Hot Afternoons in Montana." Later there began a hot polemic around that poem. Conrad Aiken came and shouted that Segal had plagiarized him. And Segal answered him, they began . . . Conrad Aiken's poem was printed, and Segal's poem.

I said, "Why didn't you say a word about any of these?" I wanted to know whether she had a low opinion of them, or . . .

She answered me very politely. "Upton Sinclair is an extreme radical." Upton Sinclair had just written his book *The Goose-Step*. That was an attack on the American universities. He wanted to show that the American universities are goose-stepping, following the line of the Establishment. So she answered me, "Upton Sinclair is a radical. I wouldn't mention a man who has written a book called *The Brass Check*."[5] Do you know what *The Brass Check* was? Upton Sinclair had written a play which was a work about prostitution in America. A *brass check* was—when someone went into one of those houses, he got a brass check to show that he had paid, and then he showed the brass check. "Anyone writing *The Brass Check* is unworthy of being mentioned."

I already saw who I was dealing with. So I said, "And what

5. *The Brass Check* was published in 1919; *The Goose-Step—A Study of American Education*, in 1923.

about the poet V. F. Calverton and his journal, you know, *The Modern Quarterly*."

She hadn't heard of it. She admitted, "I've never heard of it." The first time she'd heard of it. You understand—she lived in a world that was altogether removed from the fact that there were Trotskyists in America. She didn't know anything, Trotskyist, not Trotskyist . . .

Later the younger teachers, the liberals, said to me, "Ah, you're going to try to discuss it with her? It's like talking to Rip Van Winkle about modern technology."

I decided that it would be better for me to go to a more modern university. And I had the idea that the state universities . . . A student told me, "Wisconsin is good, it's a good university. There's a liberal spirit there, and . . ."

CN: What were your impressions of the Jewish community in Baltimore?

SN: A very interesting community. Extremely interesting. I once met a Jew there by the name of Hartog Genesis, who had come to America in the Colonial period. They came to New York. His great-great-great-grandparents came to New York when New York was still New Amsterdam, Nieuw Amsterdam. And he was a pious Jew. Had his own minyan. A wealthy Jew, an extremely wealthy Jew.

I will finish soon. One more episode in Baltimore. And here there enters a girl with whom I became acquainted, who studied at a girl's college, Goucher. I'll tell you why I mention this.

I'm going to tell you something, and you'll look at me very skeptically.

Once I got a letter from the deacon, Dean Ames, that I should come and respond to a complaint of aggravated assault on a fellow student. Can you imagine? Me? Aggravated assault? Why me?

I wanted to go see what this was about. At Hopkins there was a childish institution called hazing.

JB: There were fraternities?

SN: Yes, it was all fraternities. The first week, before the college opened, there was orientation. The freshmen had to come a week earlier. And there was someone named "Doc" Sergeant. Doc Sergeant was a sophomore. He let the freshmen know that the sophomore hazing committee had decided that the freshmen had to wear a silly cap, sort of a —

JB: Beanie.

SN: A beanie, yes, a beanie. And in addition they would have to carry two raw eggs in their pockets. I stood up immediately and said, "The beanie doesn't bother me, but the eggs: Baltimore is a big city, you know, you have to go somewhere and it's rush hour, and I'm going to wear two eggs in my pockets? It'll leak from my . . ."

I didn't wear them. I said I wouldn't wear them. And here we come to the story. One time, during Thanksgiving week, I was walking on the campus. I had been in a class, or I was going to buy books. Several guys came along — Doc Sergeant among them — pushed me and said, "Hey Freshie! Show us your eggs!"

I said, "I'm not carrying any eggs. I don't want to."

They winked at each other and — they didn't say anything to each other, but four guys came up to me and grabbed me. One on one arm, another on the other arm, the other two by my two legs, and they carried me. That didn't bother me. Let them carry me. Suddenly I saw that they were going to throw me into a pond that was nearby. I wouldn't be drowned, but I would get wet. And I had to go teach. I taught a class at four o'clock in a Talmud Torah. And I began to defend myself. Finally I managed to get one leg free and I kicked out at Doc Sergeant. You know, when you strike from here—there's a lot of strength in the knee. I kicked Doc Sergeant, and he shouted, "Ouch!" And he began to limp. The others let me go, they let me go free. He was limping, and they took him into the health service, and they took an X ray there. It was nothing. He didn't break his leg, but he limped for several days. I'd given him a really good shot, right here.

Two days later I got a letter from the dean. Dean Ames was very unfriendly. Very unfriendly. He said, "Mr. Noble, this is not American sportsmanship." He gave me a lecture. "American sportsmanship takes these things good-naturedly."

I said, "Dean Ames, I'm sorry, I didn't intend to really hurt him. I didn't know that I would—but you know, when you're struggling for your life, and there were four fellows holding me, you know, bigger boys"—it didn't take much to be bigger than myself, you know, and they were dragging me and they were going to throw me in. Perhaps they were merely saying it, and they wouldn't have thrown me in. But in any case—"I struggled, and in the struggle I kicked out, you know."

In short, he gave me a very sharp lecture. An unfriendly lecture. He said, "You'll have to understand American sportsmanship, Noble."

What are you laughing about?

CN: He thought he was more American than the students, and he should explain to them what was American and what wasn't American.

SN: Yes, yes, yes. And he said to me that it was a serious matter. "Mr. Sergeant may sue in civil court."

I would have to pay yet, and I didn't have enough to keep my body and soul together. And I stood there and repeated everything: "I'm awfully sorry. Honestly, Dean Ames. I didn't intend to hurt him. You know in the struggle—you never know, so, you get excited, I kicked out for dear life."

He said, "Your father will have to come to see me." At that time my father was in Nashua, New Hampshire. And he would have come, my father would have come.

I said, "That's impossible, Dean. My father cannot come. He simply cannot afford the trip from Nashua. It's about forty dollars."

"Well, I'm sorry," he said, "you are not of age. And besides, you should have a guardian here." I was nineteen years old.

I thought and I thought, and then I had an idea: I would ask the girl to come. I would say she was my sister. So I said, "Dean Ames, I have an older sister here in Baltimore. Could she come?"

"Is she of age?"

I said, "Yes."

"Oh," he said, "in that case, good." I have a slight suspicion that he knew that it wasn't the truth, that I had made up the story. Because when she came, he gave the two of us a sly look, and he said, "You don't look at all like siblings!" That's what he said, with a smile, but he didn't say a thing.

I spoke very little. She said, "Well, Shlomo was always a wild kid, kind of. Kind of a wild kid, you know."

The dean really thought I was kind of a killer, and he gave me another lecture, he said, "You've got to learn American sportsmanship." So how was I to learn sportsmanship? "Come to the football games."

In short, I got out of that trouble. But I decided—the year ended in Baltimore, and the year after I went off to Minnesota.

CN: Between the Jewish students at Johns Hopkins who had been in America a long time or who were born in America, and the greenhorn students, was there some tension?

SN: There weren't any greenhorn students. I was practically the only greenhorn student. In general there were very few Jewish students. In my class there was a young man with the name of Krivitsky, Shlesinger—but Shlesinger didn't say that he was a Jew, he hid himself.

But I must tell you that the other students, my friends were all Southerners. Very good students—there was Trueheart, Reynolds. Reynolds once said to me, "You know," he said, "come visit us." He invited me: "We have an estate in the South." Reynolds was from the tobacco family, Reynolds Tobacco. And he was very friendly to me. I'll tell you sometime—no, it's not important. Reynolds—and Trueheart. Trueheart's mother told me once that they wanted to adopt me, so I would have a good future, really a good future.

I said, "You know, for me to take the name Trueheart . . . It's entirely different, you know."

JB: It's not so different, from Noble to Trueheart.

The American Heartland

SN: Yes. Well—this is how I arrived in Minnesota. I decided that a state university would be a bit more modern, a bit more democratic. And I began to think perhaps Minnesota, perhaps Wisconsin, Michigan . . . I even thought of California.

I came to New York for the Sabbath. I was at a Bar Mitzvah in New York, and there I met a Conservative rabbi. He's still alive today, the oldest Conservative rabbi. He was the rabbi in St. Paul then. His name is Phillip Kleiman. We became acquainted and he asked me, "What do you do?" I told him that I had been in Baltimore for a year and now I was looking for someplace else to go . . .

He said, "Oh, would I like it if you would come study where we live, in St. Paul! We have a job for you, made to order."

We discussed it, and I said, "Yes, perhaps I would consider it." And a few days later I received a telegram, inviting me to come, detailing their offer. I accepted.

I arrived in St. Paul in September 1925. And I liked the university very much. There were very few Jewish students. That was a problem with that university. I liked it, yet I missed the Jewish ambience. I thought about it, and I began to see that I was being drawn more and more into the Gentile atmosphere. Whether I wanted to or not, I was being drawn into the Gentile sphere.

In the university I had the good fortune of meeting Professor Ross Finney,[6] a sociologist. Ross David Finney was the founder of what is called rural sociology. He argued that until then sociology had only been in the cities, urban sociology, and he began working to get them to include the sociology of small towns, of the countryside, especially in America. He was an important man. He took a great interest in me. I'll give you an illustration: He saw that I did not look well, I looked pale, and so forth. He said, "That's no good." He found out where my last class was, and he waited for me so that we could go on foot from Minneapolis to St. Paul. There was a bridge over the Mississippi. At first it was very unpleasant for me, because it was always cold, but later I became accustomed to it. And as we walked, we used to talk about various things. He told me about his life. He had been raised on a farm there. And later he began studying, received an education and became a professor, and so forth.

He suffered very much on account of the fact that he was very, very progressive for those times. For example, he said, "Just take a look. In Minnesota there are sixty or fifty courses in

6. Ross David Finney taught at the University of Minnesota during the 1920s. According to scholars I have contacted, Noble's claim that Finney was the "founder of rural sociology" seems exaggerated.

Latin. And there isn't even a single course in Russian. I told them that it was necessary to have a course in Russian. Eventually, you'll see," he said. "A time will come when there will be courses in Russian. But I won't live to see it."

I enjoyed being in his presence so much. He was so unconventional. I really responded to him.

At a certain point I began to be very interested in German literature. There was a professor there from Germany by the name of Burckhardt. I had very many long talks with Professor Burckhardt. The one question in German literature that especially interested me was why Jews were so heavily represented in postwar German Expressionism. Not only in literature, but also in theater and music. Jews, Jews, Jews. Wherever you went, Jews were prominent. And at that time I proposed the theory that avant-gardism is the result of the function of the Jews. Someone who is not so secure feels the least tremor, before someone who is sure of his position. We're sitting here: I'm sitting in the center, and you're sitting on the periphery. Someone opens the window, and a breeze blows in. It's understandable that the one who's at the periphery by the window feels it, while the one at the center won't feel it so quickly. At that time, and still now, I think that this theory stands up well, and it can explain various manifestations in literature. And I used it to explain why Expressionism was, so to speak, a function almost exclusively of Jews. I used it to explain—the poet Franz Werfel, for example, has a poem in which the wanderer calls to us. The wanderer says, "I am tired of wandering." These are people who were uprooted, displaced persons—and that's who they were in this poem. And this was around the time of the First World War.

In Minnesota, as I said, there were very few Jews. I lacked a Jewish ambience there. I got involved in Jewish cultural work then. I received a letter from Henry Hurwitz, who was at that time the editor of a very good Jewish journal called *Menorah*

Journal. There were even Menorah Societies. And he asked me to try to organize a Menorah Society there.

This was the source of a comic incident: There was a young man in my sociology class. I thought his name was Berkowitz, but he looked like a Swede. Tall, big, with blue eyes and blond hair, white-blond hair . . . And I went up to him and began asking him to become a member of the Menorah. He looked at me and said very politely, "But I'm not a Jew."

I said, "Oh, come on. With a name like Berkowitz, you're not a Jew?"

He said, "You know, I thought you were calling me Berkowitz. My name is Bergquist."

I had one other comic moment—and perhaps this moment was not so comic. There was one other Jewish student in addition to me. He was originally from Russia, but he came to Minnesota directly from Germany. He had studied at Berlin University for some time. Somehow he wasn't decent; a troubled person. Rosenberg was his name.

There was also a Christian girl named Janssen in the class. Very unattractive, an ugly girl. She was lame in one leg. And Rosenberg fell in love with her. She didn't know I was a Jew. Imagine, a name like Shlomo. Maybe they hadn't heard the name Shlomo there. Anyway, one time she said to me, "I don't know how to get rid of that Jew boy." And she began making very nasty anti-Semitic comments.

In Minnesota the honor system was in force. There was never an examination that you couldn't take according to the honor system. But it was very badly exploited. The German exam came. She approached me and said, "Can I copy?" She knew very little, a terrible student.

I very quickly filled up one of the blue books we had to write the exams in. I simply wrote foolish answers. I remember we had to cite something from Goethe, a famous bit written by Goethe. What I wrote from "Goethe" was: "*Eins, zwei, drei, vier—gib mir noch ein Glas Bier!"* / *"Sieben, acht—nicht getracht"* ("One, two, three, four, pour for me a glass of beer! / Seven eight, don't hesitate"), and so forth. And she actually copied it just as I had written it. After she left I wrote a proper exam.

The professor came back and said, "One student seems to have taken leave of his senses. There's one insane examination." But she had probably heard about it. She didn't come back. We didn't see her in class. Not in class, and not even at the university.

As I said, I had no Jewish circle, no friendship. And if I wanted to go out sometimes, I had to ask a non-Jewish girl to go, because there weren't any Jewish girls.

So I went out with a Christian girl. We went to various concerts and other functions, until one time . . . She was a girl of Norwegian descent. Her name was Skavermor. Very gentle, delicate. One time she said to me that there was one thing she'd really like to see. I asked her what that was. She said that she would really like to see—what's that called, with the bulls, in Spain?

JB: A bullfight.

SN: A bullfight. Yes, she wanted very much to go to a bullfight. And in particular she wanted to see the bull killing the matador. That's what she wanted to see. She said that to me. When I heard that, one word came into my mind: Esau. From that point on I thought, "No, I'm not going to stay in Minnesota." I decided immediately to go back.

Incidentally, while I was in Baltimore I went to New York. Somehow I met a girl here, a younger girl, very quiet and modest, who came from Prague. And the girl stayed very much in my mind. I thought of her. I didn't write to her, but I thought of her. And at the end of the year—

JB: You had met her for the first time here in New York?

SN: Yes, here in New York.[7] And at the end of the year I decided that I had thought enough about the girl, and I would travel to New York to see her. In short, that girl later became my wife.

Return to New York

SN: I left Minnesota, and decided I would stay in New York this time. I began to think about going to a school here in New York. Somehow I missed the deadline. I couldn't register at Columbia, which is where I actually wanted to go. Then I thought of City College, because I thought City College was Jewish. I went to City College then, and I had an interview with a professor named Dudley. He was a decent person. He said, "Listen to me. You're coming from Johns Hopkins. Johns Hopkins is a university where people are polite. And here people are pushy. One on top of the other." He said, "You won't be comfortable here. Think about another university."

Finally I registered at New York University. This was in the fall of 1926.

Suddenly I began to be interested in journalism. But at New York University, journalism was part of the School of Commerce, Accounts and Finance, which was a separate school. It had very, very low standards. But ultimately I registered there, and I took several courses in journalism. There I encountered anti-Semitism practically for the first time. In New York University most of the students were Jewish.

7. According to Naomi Noble Richard, Shlomo Noble and his wife were actually first cousins: Shlomo's mother Nekha was the sister of Nina's father Chaim. They had met in Europe several times, and she was from a much wealthier and more worldly family than his.

There was a professor named Lipple. And this Lipple once made the following remark. In class we happened to discuss the Eucharist. There was one Gentile girl, an Italian girl who knew what the Eucharist is. And I knew a bit about the Eucharist, but not much. He asked: "And the rest of you I suppose are"—and he cast a glance and said with a sort of smile—"Zionists."

I said to Professor Lipple, "I'm sorry. I feel that denoting me as a Zionist, denoting the rest of us as Zionists, is somehow unbecoming." We had a bit of a conflict over that issue. I quickly realized that he was indeed somewhat infected with anti-Semitism.

I transferred to Washington Square College. I liked the professors better there. I was there for two years. Actually I should have graduated by then, but because I had kept transferring from one college to the other, I wasn't given full credit. So I was still lacking quite a few points for graduation.

That year I got married. We lived in Far Rockaway, which was then far, far from the city. Almost like a village. Isolated.

CN: There was also no subway.

SN: No, no. There was no subway. You had to take the train, and so forth. And once in Far Rockaway I met a man named Dinish. He said to me, "Perhaps you would like to leave New York?"

I said, "Yes, very much." Both my wife and I were simply tired of New York City.

"There's a very good position. You could get it."

I said, "Yes."

"Not a big city. Not so little, maybe not a town: Wilkes-Barre, Pennsylvania." And so we arrived in Wilkes-Barre, Pennsylvania, in 1928. And I began thinking that I would finally have to graduate, and go to graduate school—

Pennsylvania and Ohio

SN: And there I finished. There I concentrated entirely on classics, on Latin and other languages. The school was St. Thomas Aquinas. Now it's called the University of Scranton. They changed the name, now it's just Scranton University.

When I graduated, I finally decided to study in Europe. My studies in Europe were very, very successful. I was pleased with them. But unfortunately I made a mistake. I planned to go. But the university in Zurich seemed provincial, and I decided to go to the center of Germany.[8] And that was a mistake. Because it was already close to 1932, and in 1932, Germany was already in a very, very nervous situation. The anti-Semitism, the Hitlerism, was terrible, terrible. And it was almost impossible to study at all in the universities. There were demonstrations every day.

But I held on—I thought that perhaps, perhaps . . . until September 1932. By September 1932 I could no longer stay. Naturally I myself was to blame for a number of things. I expressed myself in a very anti-Hitlerite way, of course, and the Hitlerite students were keeping an eye on me.

So in September 1932, as I said, I saw that I couldn't stay any longer. I returned to America. In Switzerland and Germany, all I had left was my dissertation. Here, of course, I still had to work for several years. First I decided that I would give up my studies, because I was very dejected when I returned from Germany. Especially when I heard that Hitler had actually come to power. That was extremely depressing for me. I didn't want to go to school.

But meanwhile I happened to hear that one of the teachers whom I knew from there had come to America. A Jew in fact, a converted Jew. Hans Sperber was the founder of semantics, of

8. Frankfurt-am-Main, in fact.

the school of semantics. I heard that he was at Ohio State. So I went to Ohio State. And that's where I finished my studies.

When I finally graduated in 1939, the chief of the department offered me a position. An instructorship with little money. But on one condition: that I should say nothing, not a word about present-day Germany. I looked at him and I said, "How could one possibly in this time, in 1939, not say something about Germany? How can one study and learn altogether without mentioning the present situation?"

He made excuses for himself, saying "You know, we are dependent on the budget of the state, and this could create, you know . . ." And it was true, I had made a few remarks—not very friendly, of course—about Hitler. And that had probably been noted somewhere, and it had probably been discussed, and they kept an eye on me.

JB: For me it's something new, that I'm only starting to learn now: how friendly official America was to Hitler. Before Pearl Harbor.

SN: Oh! The universities simply surrendered immediately. I must tell you something about the universities. They really compromised from the very beginning on.

I also studied for a year at the University of Pennsylvania. University of Pennsylvania, in 1936–37. There were, I think, about fifteen students in the graduate department. Among them were a good number of Jews. Noble, there was a Jew Epstein, there was a Jew by the name of Leshkoff, a girl, Dorothy Leshkoff, and others. And there was a question regarding a course in Middle High German—whether it should be conducted in English or in German. A show of hands was asked for. Since I had just come back from Germany, the terminology was more familiar to me in German. I voted for German. There were two Nazi exchange students—one was named Matz and one was named Peisel. And they figured that I was probably also a German.

They approached me once late in 1936. At that time the Nazi propagandist Hans Gruen had come; the author of the book *Volk ohne Raum*, which was a best-seller in Germany, came to America. *Volk ohne Raum*—that is, a people who have no land. A propaganda book.

When he came to Philadelphia, the two Nazi exchange students gave him a reception. They asked me to be on the committee. I said: "Actually, why did he come, this Hans Gruen?" At that time a German gangster had been shot in New York, Dutch Schultz. "It seems to me that the only reason he came is to eulogize that specimen of Nordic humanity, Dutch Schultz."⁹

Matz looked at me and said, *"Sind Sie Jude?"*

I didn't answer. He turned away. From that time on he didn't know me. He didn't know me anymore, that Matz.

I left Philadelphia. But Epstein, who was in class with me, told me the following story. Epstein took an exam together with Matz, a doctoral exam. At the doctoral exam there was a Jewish professor, a convert, Klarman. At the exam he asked Matz a question about Heine. Matz stood up and announced: "For me that is not part of German literature. That is part of Jewish literature. I absolutely refuse to answer the question." And all of the professors sat there, including the chair of the department, and didn't say anything.

And Klarman sat like a dead man. And he sat there a few minutes, then he looked up and said, "Well, I have no further business here." And no one said a word; the examination continued.

That's how far it went.

9. In fact, "Dutch Schultz," whose real name was Arthur Flegenheimer and who was prominent in the bootlegging industry during Prohibition, was Jewish.

SN: So that means we have finished with my education . . . And we arrive at my period at the YIVO, beginning in the year 1944.

And with that, children, I want to end, I'm in a bit of a hurry. We'll see each other—not this Friday, this Friday I have to see the doctor, but we'll see each other next Friday, yes?

JB: But—

SN: What?

JB: We're dying to hear the story about the crazy man, but if you have to go away . . .

SN: I have to go. The story is a long story. It drew out. I forgot, and then he came again. It was—suddenly he'd show up. It was bizarre—really a bizarre story. Good, I'll tell you that next Friday, a week from Friday. Be well, and I have to run. I hope I won't be late.

COMMENTARY

In these stories of his higher education, Noble describes himself growing gradually more reflective about what it means to be Jewish in America. Unlike Beaver Falls and the yeshiva in New York, here he is truly receiving an American secular education in the English language, and in the process, as he says, being progressively "drawn into the Gentile sphere"—especially before he marries his Prague-born Jewish wife. At the same time he is coming to identify himself with a very specifically modern type of alienated European Jewish intellectual, and to theorize on the basis of that experience. For someone who senses acutely his own marginality, it can be not only comforting but strengthening to develop a reflexive understanding of that situation. For Shlomo Noble, thinking about Jewish cultural history was a way of figuring out how to make his way without losing himself.

One of the most important—and perhaps hardest—lessons Noble had to learn was how to distinguish genuine discrimination from perceived discrimination. To have been overly sensitive to putative anti-Semitism would have hampered his education and his goal of achieving multicultural competence; to have overlooked actual cases of anti-Semitism would have been a betrayal of his Jewish identity. Two incidents during the year at Johns Hopkins exemplify the process through which he learned this lesson. In one, he overhears as a fellow Jewish student is gently rebuked for shouting the words "Jesus Christ!" as a curse. Thinking at first that the Jewish student has been unfairly singled out, he later decides that the censorship was attributable to the generally prudish approach toward language at Johns Hopkins at that time. In the second incident, Noble likewise suggests that the professor may have been justified in asking him to make sure he knew what words meant before he used them, since he refers back to an earlier teacher's dictum that words needn't be looked up in the dictionary, and "With guessing, you're never entirely certain that you understand." On the other hand, just in case the professor's solicitude did constitute a slur on Noble as a Jew, Trickster was careful to respond with the by now tried-and-true method of exaggerated compliance, which we have seen earlier in the cases of "Reb" Itsik and "vespers."

Noble chose not to comply with the ritual humiliation of freshmen, however. In the encounter with Doc Sergeant, Dean Ames and the threat of expulsion or a civil suit, Noble as Trickster becomes more cautious, pretending to acquiesce in the authoritative judgment of his character—"Shlomo was always kind of a wild kid"—without attempting to parody the abuse of power. In this case, discretion is the better part of valor. Yet here as well, a ruse is involved—one which seems rather transparent even to the dean himself, and which thus requires Dean Ames's collusion in order to succeed. Noble refrains from commenting on the suggestion that attendance at football games would make him more aware of the rules of sportsmanship.

Yet concern for detecting anti-Semitism is not quite the same thing as Noble's ambivalence about "America." Noble several times repeats the names of his friends Truehart and Reynolds, perhaps because he's somewhat astonished in retrospect that he was able to gain their confidence, but more likely in a justifiable pride that he was sufficiently personable to overcome the cultural and social gulf between this Jewish immigrant and the sons of the Southern gentry. Doubtless the prospect of suddenly being lifted out of the social limitations of a poor immigrant milieu was a heady one. Yet the atmosphere which those names evoke gave Noble "no pleasure." After all his wanderings and a few brushes with real anti-Semitism, Noble ultimately concludes his undergraduate education at a Catholic institution named for Saint Thomas Aquinas. But his flirtation with thorough assimilation, and with non-Jewish women, has conclusively ended with a lesson that his fundamental values and "theirs"—the hands of Esau versus the voice of Jacob—will ultimately come into conflict.

Meanwhile Noble stops to call forth another virtually forgotten world, although this time not a Jewish one. Much as he took pains to detail the efflorescence of Jewish social and political life in Sanok after World War I, Noble considers literary politics in Baltimore during the mid-1920s. There is a sharp contrast between a genteel Southern city and a radical modernist culture that is just breaking through during this period. Noble's own outsider status may have made him cautious, but he presents himself as fairly outspoken in his support of the new voices. Most remarkably, Noble's vignette of his acquaintance with H. L. Mencken shows us a character both more sympathetic and less susceptible to charges of anti-Semitism than recent journalistic accounts have suggested.

When Noble did encounter blatant anti-Semitism at the University of Minnesota, his response was at least as cruel as the provocation. His target in this incident was an easy one, since the unfortunate woman obviously hadn't bothered or managed to learn a word of German. When Noble continued studying German as a graduate student in Germany and in the United States, his response to anti-Semitism was to know German better than his detractors—a standard if ultimately futile strategy well documented by the cultural historian Sander Gilman.[10] Finally, Noble's account of the pervasive Nazi influence in American university German departments from the 1930s through World War II comes as a sobering reminder that "ivory towers," too, are part of the real world.

10. *Jewish Self-Hatred: Anti-Semitism and the Hidden Language of the Jews* (Baltimore: Johns Hopkins University Press, 1986).

8

Flayshman

CN: Why didn't the Hasidim write their stories in Yiddish? They tell the stories in Yiddish, but they write them in Hebrew.

SN: To me that is a very, very strange approach. They were told in Yiddish, but when it came to writing, people thought that whatever they wanted to be permanent, must be in *loshn koydesh*.[1] They thought that what people spoke about casually, what they narrated casually wasn't so important, but still, even the Hasidic *Toyres*[2]—the Rebbe shared his *Toyres* in what language?

CN: In Yiddish.

SN: In his Yiddish. But the *Toyres* were always recorded—when the Rebbes published them, they were recorded in *loshn koydesh*. You know, the Lubavitchers have a—have you ever heard of a

1. Literally "Holy tongue," the Hebrew and Aramaic of the Bible and Talmud.
2. Here, oral teachings.

"repeater"? I once met a Jew who told me that he had served as a repeater for the Lubavitcher Rebbe, the previous Lubavitcher Rebbe. He had a very good memory. He listened very carefully, and after the Sabbath he related the stories, when they could be written down. He related it, and the scribe wrote it down. He was a repeater, and I asked him, "Tell me something."

And he precisely—let's say, at a certain moment, he coughed. Just at the moment—

JB: When the rebbe coughed.

SN: When the rebbe coughed, and he coughed too! And a second time, he coughed again. He said, "The rebbe, may he live, coughed at that point, and it stayed with me, so I cough too."

And now we come to—have you turned it on yet?

JB: Yes, yes, yes.

SN: At last I'm going to tell you about the modern meeting I had, which is an episode running through my life, until the present day. Till the present day I haven't solved this riddle.

Let's go back to the yeshiva years. I remember all the details of this episode, I remember them letter for letter, as if it stood before my . . . But whether it was the first year I lived in New York or the second year, that I don't remember. As you already know, I lived in the yeshiva.

The building had been built quite unscientifically. It had probably been built, let's say, at the beginning of the twentieth century, perhaps the end of the nineteenth century. It had originally been built as an old folks' home.

For some particular reason the windows were quite small. You see this window? Those windows were perhaps half as wide as this window. I don't know why they made such narrow little windows. And very unscientifically built. It worked out so that

I had sun in my room nearly the entire day. All the windows faced the sun; I had sun from early in the morning until late at night. So it was terribly warm in my room. It seems to me that in general it was warmer in New York then than it is now. If you ask people, they'll say the same thing—that in the early twenties it was terribly hot in New York. It was the Sabbath. But I don't remember whether it was in 1921 or 1922. It was in summer.

I ate my Sabbath lunch, and as I've already told you, I was an extremely diligent student. After eating I always went and studied. I had a sort of principle: Once you've eaten, that is, you've taken care of the material, you have to do something for the soul.

One Sabbath it was so hot that I sat down and the Gemore was soaked with my sweat. I decided that it was impossible to study. I had to go outside somewhere to look for a bit of air. It was suffocating. The yeshiva was on East Broadway—Cannon Street.[3] Do you know the neighborhood there? Grand Street and East Broadway met there.

I took a Hebrew book. I decided to go somewhere to look for a bit of air. And I figured that if I went to the river, perhaps it would be a bit cooler. I remember exactly what the book was. It was a Hebrew journal called *Miklat*. You know what a *miklat* is? *Refuge*. It was published here in New York. It was a very good journal.

I finally found a tree near Cherry Street, by the river. I remember the story I was reading. Do you want to know the story? It was very interesting. The story was a description by Mordechai ben Yechezkel. I didn't know it then, but later I found out he was Ahad Ha'am's[4] son-in-law. He described his wartime experiences in the Russian Army.

3. Like several other streets on the Lower East Side which were close to the East River, Cannon Street no longer exists.

4. Ahad Ha'am, pen name of Asher Ginzberg (1856–1927). Zionist essayist, editor and leader of the Hibbat Zion movement.

The story itself was very strange. He was assigned to a hospital, along with another Jew. And the director of the hospital was a big anti-Semite. He said, "Ah! They don't like to work. I'll give you," he said, "an easy job. At night, after people have died in the course of the day, you'll take the corpses away, lay them on a wagon, take them out into the forest, and there will be workers in the forest. They'll dig a pit, and they'll place them there. An easy job for you."

Yes, an easy job. But the other Jew was a real coward. He was afraid of approaching a corpse. And he was supposed to go up to the corpses, put them on the wagon and ride with them. He did it, he did it, but one time he went mad. At night, instead of driving to the forest, he drove to a nearby town. Drove in with a wagonload of corpses. He drove all night, and he sang. And whoever tried to talk to him, "What are you doing?" he was entirely oblivious. He just went crazy.

That's the story I was reading.

I'm sitting there reading the story, and a man comes along. He looked altogether like a Gentile, this man. I would have sworn he was a Gentile. Tall . . . And a very, very coarse face. On the right side of his face there was a scar, along the entire length of the cheek. From here to here. And he gave the impression of a somewhat nasty man. Very coarse. He sat down next to me. And strange—he looked into the book I was reading, the Hebrew book. I figured, "Ah, it's just curiosity. He wonders what I'm reading." I said nothing.

Suddenly he said to me in bad Hebrew: "*Adoyni mayven beivris?*" Do you understand what that means?

CN: He asked if you understand Hebrew.

SN: I answered in Hebrew as well. I said, "Since I read, I probably understand as well."

He said nothing. I kept reading. And later he started talking to me, still in bad Hebrew. He asked me in Hebrew, "Have you been in America long?"

I said, "A year." I don't remember exactly whether it was a year, or whether it was a bit longer . . .

And he asked me, "Where do you come from?"

I said, "From Poland."

So I asked him. If he was asking me—"Where do you come from?"

"From Amsterdam."

This was interesting to me. A Jew from Amsterdam, looks like a criminal. Looked exactly like a criminal. And we spoke a bit more, and he said, "You're precisely the person I need. Precisely the person God sent to me." He introduced himself to me. He said, "My name is Avrom Flayshman."

I said, "My name is Shloyme." Good—we knew each other's names.

And he said, "You're just the person I need. Just the person."

I said, "Why do you need precisely me?"

He said, "Listen." And this was true, I knew it. At that time Dr. Thon came from Poland. Have you ever heard of Dr. Thon, Dr. Yeshue Thon?[5] He was the founder of the Tarbut movement. Do you know what the Tarbut movement was? The Hebrew school movement. Tarbut. And he came to America to collect money for Tarbut, and he used the opportunity to open a branch of Tarbut in New York, for higher Hebrew studies. And I even still remember the address. It was at 128 Stanton Street. That's where their school was. I said, "And what do you want?"

He said, "I want to enter the school. But in order to enter the school one has to write an autobiography of two thousand five hundred words." Two thousand five hundred—a substantial autobiography.

5. Osias Thon (1870–1936), rabbi of Cracow, member of the Polish parliament (Sejm) and Zionist cultural leader.

JB: In Hebrew.

SN: In Hebrew. He said, "On the basis of this biography either one is accepted or rejected. I certainly cannot write such a long autobiography, but you can write the biography for me, and I will pay you."

I agreed. So I had to write the biography. "When do you need it?"

"This evening," he said. "Right after Havdalah[6] you have to begin writing." He said, "I don't live far from here." He lived, I think, either on Madison Street or on Monroe Street, one of those streets. He said, "I have a room. We can work there. Right after Havdalah we'll begin." And we spoke a bit more, and then I realized it was time to go to *shales-sudes*.[7] I said, "Perhaps you'd like to come eat *shales-sudes* with me?"

He said, "Yes." He didn't want to leave me. We shared whatever there was to eat, and shortly after we made Havdalah, and we went off to his rooms. He had a small room, but there was space for two people to work. He sat down on the bed, and I sat on a cushion, and he began recounting.

He began thus: *Noladati*—I was born; *bekfar bebavaria*—he was born in a village in Bavaria. This surprised me: in the Alps? All the same, a man can be born anywhere, why not? Born in a village in Bavaria. He told me that when he was three years old, his mother died. And two years later his father died. A strange thing . . . "But don't mention this," he said at certain places; he just wanted to explain it to me. "I don't want you to write that, because they won't accept me if you write this down." His mother was a Jewish girl. His father wasn't a Jew, the father was a Gentile, a Christian, a Catholic. After his father died, his father's father took him into his home. His grandfather was a Bavarian peasant, and that's where he grew up.

6. The ceremony marking the end of the Sabbath and the beginning of the week.
7. The ritual "third meal" on Saturday afternoon.

He continued dictating. He said, "I received my earliest education from the village priest."

I stopped at that point. I said, "What, you received your earliest education from the priest?"

He explained it to me: "My father wasn't a Jew. My grandfather wasn't a Jew either. And since my mother . . . " He didn't want to talk about his mother. I don't know why. All he told me was that his mother had been Jewish. He knew she was Jewish, because she kept up certain Jewish customs. He told me he remembered that his mother had lit candles Friday night.

He continued. There were a few Jewish families there. And a slaughterer from Munich used to come every Thursday. Every Thursday the slaughterer came. The slaughterer would kill poultry for the Jews, and sometimes even a calf, if there was some sort of affair. The slaughterer became acquainted with the boy, and tried to become friendly with him. When he came every Thursday, he would bring chocolate and so forth for the boy, and he spoke with him. They became very close. The boy would anticipate the slaughterer's arrival, and when the slaughterer came they spent time together . . .

One day the slaughterer asked, "Do you know that you're a Jewish boy?"

The boy said, "Yes, I know. I know that—I remember that my mother was Jewish." But the Jewish boy was in a completely Gentile atmosphere. He went to a Catholic school.

The slaughterer began telling him a bit about Jews, and once he asked quite openly: "Do you want to become a Jew again? I will take you where there are Jews," he said, and "you'll become a Jew."

And since the slaughterer had given him chocolate and other good things, the boy thought that it was good to be a Jew. He said so. The boy was probably six or seven years old then, because he could write a bit; and perhaps a bit older. I don't know exactly, because I didn't record it. The boy said, "Yes."

The slaughterer said, "I'll take you far away, among Jews, and you'll be a Jew. And I'll see to it that you get a home." And the slaughterer really kidnapped the boy. It was not far from the border, and they crossed over into Austria. He stopped there. He took the boy to an inn.

Meanwhile there arose a great big hullabaloo in Germany, in Bavaria, in the village. A child, a Christian child, had disappeared. A Christian child disappeared, you understand? And one newspaper, an anti-Semitic newspaper which was published in Germany at that time, the *Kreuzzug*—you know what *Kreuzzug* means?

JB: Yes, the *Crusade*.

SN: *Crusade*. The *Kreuzzug*, that's what it was called, a Catholic Christian newspaper.

JB: This was around the year 1890?

SN: No, no. It was around the year 1906–7-8, approximately.

JB: So this person wasn't much older than you.

SN: No, no, no, no, no, no, no. Not much older than me. Probably about five years older. Maybe a little more. I don't know exactly.

Anyway, the *Kreuzzug* even hinted that what was involved was a ritual kidnapping. And there was an intense search. Not only in Bavaria, but all over Germany. And they even began searching in Austria. The German police asked the Austrian police to look for the child. The slaughterer became afraid and took the child with him across the entire length of Austria, to the city of Brod. And why Brod?

CN: On the Russian border.

SN: On the Russian border. Brod is a large city, a commercial city, people come there and people go there, there's always a lot of strange people in Brod. Perhaps they might not look for him there. And the slaughterer was with the child there for a long time. And they lived with a Jewish family there. Apparently the family knew about the fact that the child wasn't the slaughterer's own, but . . . they began searching in Brod as well. I don't know if they really did, or if the slaughterer just became afraid that they would come search in Brod as well, that they'd start asking questions in Brod.

He took the boy and crossed across the border into a city called Radziwilow. (And about Radziwilow you know because my father was a soldier in Radziwilow during the war years. At that time my father was still alive; I asked him, and he said everything was correct.) And there the slaughterer gave the child to a rich Jewish family which had no children. I don't know who they were. And the slaughterer left. The boy was left alone there in Radziwilow. He lived thoroughly as a Jew. He went to a Jewish heder . . .

CN: Had he been circumcised?

SN: Yes, his mother had insisted he be circumcised.

Not long later—I asked him how much later, he said he didn't remember exactly, but a few years later—the war broke out, and he left Radziwilow. I don't know how, whether with someone, or . . . it isn't clear to me. Even at that time it wasn't clear to me. Somehow, in the midst of the war, he left Radziwilow and came to Amsterdam. There in Amsterdam he lived again with a Jewish family. And from Amsterdam, he came here. In Amsterdam he received a very good Jewish education. I've told you about the bit of Hebrew he'd gotten in Amsterdam.

And with that ended the story that I wrote. And—do we still have time?

JB: Yes, yes.

SN: Good. Let me know when we have to stop.

JB: No—it's the machine that lets us know.

SN: Yes—when the machine lets us know.

There he was in New York. I finished writing, and he gave me a five dollar bill. It was a large sum, but I worked until two o'clock in the morning, until it was finished. He didn't want to let me go. I had to finish.

I thanked him, and I went back to my room. A few days later he came and said that they had accepted him. He had handed in the application, handed in the autobiography, and they accepted him. And he learned very well there. He learned a lot of Hebrew in the Tarbut School . . .

But one thing wasn't clear to me. What did he live on? Such things, you know, one cannot ask. Where did he have money to live on? He told me that he had worked for a short time when he arrived, but at that time he was studying full time.

He used to come visit me in the yeshiva. Once he came to visit me and he said he had met a doctor named Moyshe Einhorn. I knew Dr. Einhorn. He had an office not far from here, Park Avenue. Einhorn was a specialist in stomach diseases. Dr. Einhorn had hired him as a private teacher for his children. He gave him his own room in the house, and later Einhorn took in some other doctors' children, his colleagues' children, and he had a sort of small private school there in his house. And apparently he was doing well, because he was very well dressed, and he said that he lived in Dr. Einhorn's house.

SN: Some time passed since he had moved uptown, and I didn't see him so often. Every two or three months he used to come see me. And at the end of that year I left New York for Baltimore, from Baltimore to Minnesota, from Minnesota I came back to New York, but the whole time I forgot about him completely. And he probably forgot about me.

And that's Chapter One. There ends the "New York" chapter of Avrom Flayshman.

Meanwhile I got married, I went away, studied in Europe, the Nazis came, I started studying here again in America, and I was working then on my dissertation about *khumesh-taytsh*.[8]

I used to work in the Jewish Division of the Public Library. At that time Dr. Yehoshue Bloch was the librarian there. I'd hand in a list of books, and he prepared the books for me, he helped me a great deal. And I often worked in the Jewish Division . . . This is Chapter Two.

Once, it was either 1936 or 1937, I was sitting in the Jewish Division. A man walked in. I looked at him. It was Avrom Flayshman. Of course, I got up and walked over to him, and greeted him: "*Sholem-aleykhem*, Avrom Flayshman!"

He said, "I don't know you."

I said, "My name is Noble, Shlomo Noble. You know, we were once quite . . ."

And after I talked awhile . . . "Oh, yes, yes. I remember now. Yes, yes, yes," he said, "now I remember. Shloyme Noble. You know, I now live in Palestine. I've been in Eretz Yisroel quite a few years, and I've changed my name. My name is no longer Avrom Flayshman," and instead he gave me some Hebrew name. You know, the kind of modern Hebrew name, like all the . . .[9]

8. The particular idiom of Yiddish traditionally used for phrase-by-phrase instructional translations of the Bible.

9. It was customary throughout most of this century for new immigrants to the Jewish settlement in Palestine, and then to Israel, to adopt Hebrew names as a sign of their rejection of the Diaspora.

And he gave me a calling card. His name was printed on it. And it said that he was in the real estate business. He said to me that he had been very successful in Eretz Yisroel. "Thank God, it's going very well for me there." He took a picture out of his wallet, and showed me a picture of a very beautiful woman, two children, a boy and a girl. And he said to me, "I beg you, if you come to Eretz Yisroel, and probably you will—sooner or later everyone comes to Eretz Yisroel—be our guest. I have a very comfortable house, a large apartment. Thank God," he said, "things are going well for me. When you come to Eretz Yisroel, you'll visit me."

We didn't talk a long time. He talked about himself. He mentioned several times that he was rich. He said he was very satisfied, and he asked, "What are you doing?"

I said, "The same as before. I'm studying. I was in Europe for a time. I didn't finish my studies, and I want to finish them here."

We said goodbye to each other. It was a Friday afternoon. And I returned home. I didn't travel to Eretz Yisroel then, and I didn't see him.

Another twelve or thirteen years passed. I forgot. Chapter Two is a short one, and I forgot.

And in 1949 the Jewish Theological Seminary asked me to be a visiting professor at the University of Judaism in Los Angeles.

At first I had no desire, but they kept asking me, so I traveled there and I became a visiting professor. When I arrived there, I found that they had a Hebrew study circle. And this group asked me to give a lecture. My theme was "Bilingualism in Jewish History." Hebrew and Aramaic, you know, Hebrew and Arabic, a sort of summary of the . . . There was a large crowd. Really, I hadn't expected it. They had to make special arrangements, and it was overflowing, people were standing above, below . . . It was a Saturday night. It started at eight o'clock, and it was supposed to end, I guess, no later than ten. But at the end there started to be questions and discussions, and questions and discussions. I took a look, and it was already after midnight. And people were still standing, and they were absolutely demanding that I provide an answer. Amazing! Suddenly I saw a tall man with a scar across his face. He approached me. He knew my name. He said to me, *"Sholem-aleykhem."* And he said to me, "Do you know me?" In Hebrew, in good Hebrew this time.

I said, "Of course." And then I remembered his Hebrew name. "Oh yes," I said, "you're so-and-so." And I said his Hebrew name.

He looked and looked at me, and then he said, "You are mistaken."

"So who are you?"

He said, "I am Avrom Flayshman."

Now I was confused. You understand, children? "But I'm sure of it." Was I mistaken? I said, "What's going on here? What's going on here?"

He said, "My dear friend, you have confused two separate people. I have never been in Eretz Yisroel. I have no wife. I did not marry. I have no children."

But I didn't have the calling card, I had lost it somewhere. I remained confused. What's going on here? Who's the one who's not all together here—me or him? Furthermore, he didn't let me go. He was something of a *nudnik*.[10] When he stuck to you it was hard to get rid of him. And it was already one o'clock in the morning. And in Los Angeles it's hard to get a taxi, it's hard to get a bus—there's no public transportation.

He said, "Don't worry, don't worry. I have my automobile here. I've already thought of it. I'll take you home." And he came along in a very beautiful automobile, a very elegant automobile. I think it was actually a Rolls-Royce. "Get in, and I'll take you home. Where do you live?" he asked.

And I said, "Normandy Boulevard."

10. A bore or pest.

We rode along, and the whole time he told me that things were going very well for him, he was rich, very rich. But he didn't tell me what he did. He still didn't tell me what he did. Whether he was in the oil business . . . I asked him, and he said, "Oh, various businesses. I have various interests."

We stopped in front of my house. The Seminary had given me a hotel apartment, as they call it, in the Normandy Hotel. The Normandy Hotel is right on Wilshire Boulevard. He didn't want to go. It was almost two o'clock in the morning. I could barely stand up from exhaustion. And he stood there talking to me about all sorts of things. I said again, "It's strange, I remember very well that you gave me some Hebrew name . . ."

He said, "It's another person. You've confused two people."

I said "Good night." I went to bed, but all night I couldn't sleep. But finally day came, it was fully light out, and I fell asleep. And then I woke up again. Suddenly the doorbell rang. It was between nine and ten o'clock in the morning. I thought to myself, "Who's ringing so early? I don't know anyone here . . ." Who do you think was at the door? It was Avrom Flayshman, or, *alias*—the Hebrew name he had. He said to me that he had come to take me out to breakfast.

I remember we went to The Brown Derby. Perhaps you've heard of it. There's a building there that looks like a brown derby. It was very expensive. I remember it cost, at that time, two or three dollars for breakfast. And he was quite generous.

"Perhaps," he said, "you'd like to see my apartment?"

"By all means," I said.

He said, "Come, I'll show you it to you." The apartment was near Sunset Boulevard. That's a rich neighborhood, and he had a very beautiful apartment there. Very fine, elegantly furnished and all. He still wasn't telling me where he got his money. But we chatted and chatted, until he said, "Come, let's go eat supper." And he took me out again. I didn't even want to go, it was too much. He insisted that I go with him. I asked him again about his money. And he answered me again, "Various businesses." Well, "various businesses" can mean anything; everything is "various businesses."

At the same time I became acquainted with a worthy Jew, a fine, elderly man. A principal in a Hebrew school there. Reb Aron Tanis. He was a rabbi. He had been ordained by the Slobodke Yeshiva. I used to go to his house. And I hadn't yet told him anything about this Avrom Flayshman.

Avrom Flayshman, meanwhile, came to me every day, and asked me to have either supper or lunch with him. It began to be a bit too much. At a certain point I told the story to Reb Aron Tanis. "You know," he said, "somehow this story that you're telling me is an unpleasant one. Either he's not in his right mind, this person, it's a kind of amnesia, or the split personality, Dr. Jekyll and Mr. Hyde . . . You shouldn't see him anymore. Who knows what this person could do?"

Well—but he came of his own accord. Once he approached me with a plan. "You've seen my apartment"—and it was true, there was one room which was entirely empty. Finely furnished, a bedroom, and no one slept there. He said, "I'll give you that room. It won't cost you a thing. How much do you pay here?" He knew how much the rent was. He said, "I'll save you a hundred dollars a month. Tell the Seminary to give you the money, and you'll obtain lodgings for yourself."

At first I thought, "Yes, it makes sense. I can save a hundred dollars." But soon I began to have second thoughts. That evening I was at Tanis's house, and I told him the story.

Tanis said to me, "Friend Noble, you shouldn't do it. Heaven forbid! You shouldn't do it."

Why? He didn't want to say why openly, just, "I have a very good reason why you shouldn't do that. And now I understand the reason why he wants to live with you." I didn't understand.

So I said to Tanis, "What's the reason?"

He said, "He is involved in some affairs that aren't kosher.

And he wants to use you as a cover. What do you need it for, Shlomo? You'll be alone in the house, and someone will come in with a revolver, and he'll think that you're Flayshman, and he'll shoot you."

I dismissed it. But nevertheless it worked its way into my head. And I began giving Flayshman excuses. "Here," I said, "I can walk. I walk a block, and I'm already at the college. But if I'm there, I'll have to ride to the college and back."

"It doesn't matter," he said. "I'll take you there every time and I'll bring you back every time."

I began to think that Rabbi Tanis was right. I absolutely had to refuse. Meanwhile he came over practically every day, until I told him. Once he came to me with a very beautiful metal plaque that he had made: "Dr. Shlomo Noble and Abraham Flayshman," to nail to the door. "See," he said, "I've got the plaque ready. Well, come, let's get you packed and we'll move."

I thought awhile, and became very cross, grew angry, I don't know whether at myself or at him . . . I said to him, "My dear friend, I won't move. I'm going to continue living where I am, in this hotel. I'm not going to move in with you. And I'd like to ask you another thing. Come here a bit less. You come too often. I have no time, really . . ." I told him I had to prepare my lectures, I had to read, I had to work, and he took up so much time . . .

I couldn't judge his reaction. He didn't say anything. We talked a bit, and then he got up and left. And in fact he didn't call me anymore, and he didn't come anymore.

That's Chapter Three.

I was not in good health in Los Angeles, and after a few months I had to come back to the city, to New York. He didn't know anything about it. I left, and that was it.

Mrs. Tanis came to visit me once. She told me, "You know, Flayshman left his apartment. Left everything as it was, furniture, everything . . . and he went away. No one knows where he went, just that he went somewhere."

I said, "Did he leave debts?"

"No, he didn't leave any debts. He paid all his debts, paid his rent. He hasn't been seen in the city for a few weeks."

I said, "What does it mean?"

She said, "In Los Angeles, when a person disappears, it's not a good sign."

Well, nothing. I thought that it was good that I didn't get involved and live together with him.

Several years passed. In 1956 I was at Massad, a Hebrew-speaking camp. I was there for the summer, and one Saturday I was talking to the director, Dovid Eliach. Now Dovid Eliach is the principal of the Yeshiva of Flatbush.[11] We were talking about strange people, unusual people whom we had met. I told him the story of this person, as far as I knew. Mrs. Tanis had told me that he had disappeared somewhere, and that was it.

I told the story, and Dovid Eliach listened to the story very attentively. He was in utter suspense. And when I finished, he said to me, "Listen: Just tell me, does he have a scar, like this, across his entire face?"

I said, "Yes."

"And he has a kind of angry look?"

I said, "Yes, he has an angry look, he's tall, he's broad with a broad mug . . ."

He said, "Do you want to see him?"

I said, "I could see him? Yes, certainly I'd like to see him."

"Come with me. I'll show him to you."

I said, "Where is he?"

He said, "Where is he? Go to the headquarters of the Luba-vitcher Rebbe. Your man sits in the study house there from

11. A prominent modern Orthodox grade school and high school, oriented toward Hebrew and Zionism, which still exists in Brooklyn.

morning until they close it, late in the evening. Every day. They call him 'the strange one, the weird person.' He doesn't say a word. He takes a Gemore—opens it, never turns a page, looks at it and sits, looks and thinks, thinks, thinks . . . They never see him eating. Nobody sees him eating. They don't know whether he ever eats. Probably he goes out somewhere and eats something. Do you want to see him?"

First I said, "Yes. I want to see him." And later he came and said, "Come, we'll go."

Now I said no. I was afraid of the man. This time I began to fear the man. Somehow—I thought to myself, No, I won't go see him. He was a psychopath, and he might tell some sort of wild story about me, you know—that I owe him money, that I was a partner in his affairs, who knows what a person can say? I was simply afraid, and I said to Dovid Eliach, "No, I won't go."

And I never saw that person again. The story ends there.

JB: You have to leave?

SN: I have to leave.
Is there enough to finish?

JB: We have one minute.

SN: Good, we'll just end with this: What do you think of this person? What is your opinion of this person? The story that he told me, and that I wrote down—do you think that was a true story, or was it his own fantasy? And what did he want of me?

COMMENTARY

It is memory itself that seems to play tricks here. The issues of
orality and textuality—their different modes of reliability and de-
ception—weave themselves in and out of the narrative even more
explicitly than they have in the earlier chapters. And the very possibility of a consistent personal identity throughout a lifetime spent
in the modern world—Noble calls this his "modern meeting"—
comes into question.

Usually we think of written evidence as a reliable historical
source, and of oral testimony as fickle, changing according to the
situation of its transmission and the motivations of the witness. But
the preface to the story of "Flayshman" is an ethnographic thumb-
nail sketch of a situation in which oral discourse is handed down
entirely verbatim—the Lubavitch "repeater" who mentally records
the Rebbe's speech for transcription after the Sabbath. That vignette from Lubavitch is ironically echoed at the end of the chapter, when the narrative returns to Lubavitch headquarters—but
this time only to show us a visual picture of a man who sits silent
and motionless all day, in front of a book that he opens but doesn't
bother to read. In any case, the description of the repeater's professional exactitude serves to heighten the contrast both with Avrom
Flayshman's autobiography "as told to" Shlomo Noble, and with
Noble's account of his encounter with the man who only sometimes is Avrom Flayshman.

The tale of a child born to a Jewish mother and a Christian
father, raised by the father and then "kidnapped" back into a Jewish milieu is not the only story within this story. There is also the
piece in the Hebrew journal that Noble is reading when he meets
Avrom Flayshman for the first time, itself based on Mordechai ben
Yechezkel's memories of experiences in the Russian Army during
World War I. That tale certainly helps set an ominous, *noir*, modern tone for this chapter, dealing with wagons full of corpses and
the descent into flight and madness which they provoke. Note that
this is an inversion of the usual writer's technique of setting a
"told" story within a written narrative, as in Sholem Aleichem's

"The Station at Baranovitsh." Here the tone is set by relating a narrative the storyteller had been reading at the time his story began.

Noble envisioned this portion of his narrative in written form— not only the writing that I might someday make of it, but as an imaginary manuscript inside himself, which he remembered, as he says, "letter for letter." Even the structure of his telling borrows the form of the autobiographies he discusses at the beginning. The various episodes in this encounter, spanning several decades of Noble's life in America, are described as chapters: "Another twelve or thirteen years passed. I forgot. Chapter Two is a short one, and I forgot." Not only Noble's retelling, but what he remembers is influenced by what he reports having written; apologizing for a vague point in his retelling of Avrom Flayshman's autobiography, he explains, "I don't know exactly, because I didn't record it." What was written was inscribed in Noble's memory, while what was merely told, "off the record," failed to register.

Furthermore, what Noble has already told us—and what I have recorded for eventual transcription—becomes evidence against which the veracity of Flayshman's story could be checked. A geographical marker—the name of the city "Radziwilow"—is the key here. The town appears first in Noble's account of his father's war experiences, in the course of which Noble's father was interrogated about his own knowledge of the town. Here that earlier episode serves to confirm that Flayshman actually knew Radziwilow: "And about Radziwilow you know because my father was a soldier in Radziwilow during the war years. At that time my father was still alive; I asked him, and he said everything was correct." The cross-referencing thus occurs on many levels: first when the Ukrainian official checks out Noble's father's story; second when Noble checks Flayshman's story against his father's; and third when Noble offers his own retelling of his father's story as evidence for Flayshman.

This reference back to the Old World, and back to an earlier part of the narrative, is especially important in an account which ranges so wildly through chronology and geography. The story begins on the Lower East Side, moves back to various parts of Central Europe, to

New York, to Palestine, to Los Angeles and back. It mixes in references as varied as German anti-Semitic blood libels (ironically, in this
case a "Christian" child really had been kidnapped!) and fashionable
California in the mid-twentieth century. Nor, despite the protagonist's distinctive physical appearance and ultimate acknowledgment
of Noble in each "chapter," does his identity remain consistent: the
child becomes Avrom Flayshman, eventually loses that name for a
modern Hebrew pseudonym, and then returns to Avrom Flayshman,
denying that he had ever been in Palestine. Given these evident in-
consistencies, no wonder that Noble expressed skepticism about the
story he himself had written down.

The coda to the tale of Avrom Flayshman serves as a fit ending
to Trickster's entire narrative: "The story that he told me, and that
I wrote down—do you think that was a true story, or was it his own
fantasy?" Perhaps it is too convenient to assert that Noble, in asking for our evaluation of a story he recorded as told to him, was
challenging us to question his own account. But it is clear that his
narrative loses its shape in the two sessions that followed this story,
and which I have decided to leave out of the published version.
The rest is documentation—almost as if to say that the story was
ended and there was no more to say, Noble devoted much of the
last session to an overly detailed description of two cases of plagia-
rism he had encountered in his career as an editor. Even more
striking, when I interrupted to ask him to reflect on his scholarly
career and his life as a whole, he did not respond at all.

The modern meeting, then, is the climax of this tale. A psycho-
analyst might say that Flayshman was Noble's alter ego. The questions he embodied were: What makes a person a Jew? What makes
a Jew a person? Contained within the tale of Flayshman is the suggestion that this character could not integrate his identity, that he
was suffering from "either . . . amnesia or the split personality."
For an immigrant Jewish scholar such as Shlomo Noble—who
moved from a Hasidic boyhood to a worldly education in the patri-
cian South and the all-American Midwest—the appeal of either
forgetting his origins entirely, or divorcing his personality from his
scholarship, must have been great. He successfully resisted both of
those temptations, and the fruit of his struggle for integrity is the
story you have read.

Index

New Perspectives: Jewish Life and Thought

Berel Lang, series editor

A Small Place in Galilee:
Religion and Social Conflict in an Israeli Village
Zvi Sobel

A Storyteller's Worlds:
The Education of Shlomo Noble in Europe and America
Jonathan Boyarin

The Midrashic Woman
Judith Baskin

Jewish Writing in the Eye of the Inquisition
Colbert Nepaulsingh